PHARMACEUTICAL MARKETING
(For UG/PG/GPAT STUDENTS)

Other Related Books

Title	Author
Analytical methods for Medicinal Plants and Economic Botany	*M. Daniel*
Anubhut Ayurveda Chikitsa	*R.K. Bhutya*
Basic Statistics 2nd Edition	*P.K. Mohanty*
Colour Atlas of Medicinal Plants	*R.K. Bhutya*
Controversial Herbal Drugs of Ayurveda	*Amritpal Singh Saroya*
Dictionary of Local-Botanical Names in Indian Folk Life	*V. Jain*
Ethnic Indian Plants in Cure of Diabetes	*S.K. Sood*
Handbook of Legumes of World Economic Importance	*J.A. Duke*
Herbal Technology: Recent Trends and Progress	*M. Daniel*
Herbs of Tribal Land Jharkhand, India	*M.K. Jaipuriar*
Herbs: Culinary, Medicinal, Aromatic Secrets and Human Happiness	*R.K. Sud*
Materia Medica	*H.G. Greenish*
Medical Ayurvedic Dictionary (Hindi-Hindi-English-English)	*R.K. Bhutya*
Medicinal Plants of India Vol. 1-3 (Set)	*Dinesh Jadhav*
Orchids of Eastern Ghats (India)	*Kothareddy Prasad*
Orchids Of Tamil Nadu (India)	*Subbiah Karuppusamy*
Pathological Investigation with Analysis	*M.M. Dashora*
Pharmaceutical Quality Assurance	*B.P. Nagori*
Phenolic Antioxidants and Health Benefits	*U.D. Chavan*
The Green Pharmacy	*J.A. Duke*
The Medicinal and Poisonous Plants of India	*J.F. Caius*
Traditional Folk Veterinary Medicines	*S.S. Katewa*
Vanaspati Sabdkosh 2nd Edition (Hindi-Latin-English)	*S.K. Jain*

PHARMACEUTICAL MARKETING

(For UG/PG/GPAT STUDENTS)

Written by

Dr.R.N.PAL

M.Pharm, Ph.D, MBA Professor
(Formerly QA Manager,
Emami Group of Companies)

SCIENTIFIC
PUBLISHERS

Published by

SCIENTIFIC PUBLISHERS (INDIA) 5 A,
New Pali Road, P.O. Box 91 Jodhpur 342 001
(INDIA)
E-mail: info@scientificpub.com
Website: http://www.scientificpubonline.com

Print 2026

ISBN: 978-93-92590-76-4

ISBN: 978-93-92590-82-5 (EBook)

Printed in India

SYLLABUS

Scope of Pharmaceutical Marketing

Unit I

Chapter 1: Marketing: Definition, general concepts and scope of marketing; Distinction between marketing and selling; Marketing environment; Industry and competitive analysis; analyzing consumer buying behavior; Industrial buying behavior.

Chapter 2: Pharmaceutical marketing: Quantitative and qualitative aspects; size and composition of the market; Demographic descriptions and socio-psychological characteristics of the consumer; market segmentation & targeting consumer profile; Motivation and prescribing habits of the physician; patients' choice of physician and retail pharmacist. Analyzing the market: Role of market research.

Unit II

Chapter 3: Product decision: Meaning, Classification, product line and product mix decisions, product life cycle, product portfolio analysis; product positioning; New product decisions: Product branding, packaging and labeling decisions, Product management in pharmaceutical industry.

Unit III

Chapter 4: Promotion decision: Meaning and methods, determination of promotional mix, promotional budget; An overview of personal selling, advertising , mail, journals, sampling, retailing, medical exhibition, public relations, online promotional techniques for OTC Products.

Unit IV

Chapter 5: Pharmaceutical marketing channels: Designing channel, channel members, selecting the appropriate channel, conflict in channels, physical distribution management: Strategic importance, tasks in physical distribution management.

Chapter 6: Professional sales representatives (PSR): Duties of PSR, purpose of detailing, selection and training, supervising, norms for customer calls, motivating, evaluating, compensation and future prospects of the PSR.

Unit V

Chapter 7: Pricing: Meaning, importance,objectives, determinants of price, pricing methods and strategies, issues in price management in pharmaceutical industry.An overview of DPCO (Drug Price Control Order) and NPPA (National Pharmaceutical Pricing Authority).

Chapter 8: Emerging concepts in marketing: Vertical & Horizontal Marketing; Rural Marketing; Consumerism; Industrial Marketing; Global marketing.

PREFACE

Pharmaceutical marketing is the fundamental and important subject of Pharmacy Education and Research. It deals with understanding the pharmaceutical marketing and customers' behavior. Most of the pharmacy students prefer their profession as medical representative. In this regard I can say this book will do a lot of help for career building for pharmaceutical students.

This book has been written in accordance with the new syllabus prescribed by pharmacy council of India. Since the subject is altogether new to the pharmacy students,every effort has been made to deal withsubject matter in simpleand lucid languages.

Attempt has been made to make the book as informative and exhaustive as possible within constrains of time allotted to thesubject. At the end of each chapter case study is given for application of the acquired knowledge.

I made a humble attempt to present the subject in understandable languages and have taken all humble care to avoid mistakes, still if any mistake found in this book by readers may please be brought to my notice for improvement.

I thank my all colleagues, friends and my wife and daughter for their fullsupport.

Rabindranath Pal.
Pal.rabindranath@gmail.com

CONTENTS

UNIT–III

UNIT–IV

UNIT–V

SCOPE OF PHARACEUTICAL MARKETING

In the early twentieth century pharmaceutical industry was not well recognized as a complete market like other industries. At that time there were no antibiotics, no corticoids, no tranquilizer, no hypertensive, no anti-histaminicmedicins.Only a few sulpher drugs and a few vitamins were present. Even there were no oral contraceptives drugs, no effective oral anti-diabetic drugs, no prophylactic drug for gout, and no potent active oral diuretics. More over people do not heard the names of drugs to lowering the level of blood lipid and cholesterol in plasma, vaccines against polio, measles or mumps.

Now a days everyone recognizes this pharmaceutical market as self and well developed field of marketing system making these drugs available at the right time, at right place , at reasonable prices, at necessary quantities with right information. This market was controlled by overseas countries, but now this is almost fully controlled by our own country. Not only that we are also exporting some medicines to various developed and under developed countries.

This pharmaceutical market is diversified into various specialized fields like pharmaceutical dosage form, diagnostics kits and medical devices producing units. Pharmaceutical dosage forms again divided as general medicines, medicines for antihypertensive drugs, and for antibiotics drugs.

The pharmaceutical industry in India ranks 3rd in the world terms of volume and 14th in terms of value. According to Department of Pharmaceuticals, Ministry of Chemicals and Fertilizers, the total turnover of India's pharmaceuticals industry between October 2017 and September 2018 was US$61.04 billion. Hyderabad, Mumbai, Bangalore and Ahmedabad are the major pharmaceutical hubs of India. The domestic market was worth US$21.8 billion in 2018.India's biopharmaceutical industry clocked a 17 per cent growth with revenues of Rs.137 billion ($3 billion) in the 2007-18 financial year over the previous fiscal. Bio-pharmaceutical was the biggest contributor generating 60 per cent of the industry's growth at Rs.8,829crore, followed by bio-services at Rs.2,639 crore and bio-agri at Rs.1,936 crore.Exports of pharmaceuticals products from India increased in a rapid way, a combined annual growth rate of 21.25%. Some of the major pharmaceutical firms are SunPharmaceuticals, Cadila Healthcare and Piramal Enterprises

Indian companies are also starting to adapt their product development processes to the new environment. For years, firms have made their ways into the global market by researching generic competitors to patented drugs and following up with litigation to challenge the patent. This approach remains untouched by the new patent regime and looks to increase in the future. However, those that can afford it have set their sights on an even higher goal: new molecule discovery. Although the initial investment is huge, companies are lured by the promise of hefty profit margins and thus a legitimate competitor in the global industry. Local firms have slowly been investing more money into their R&D programs or have formed alliances to tap into these opportunities.

Market, Marketing and Pharmaceutical Marketing

Acommon use of the 'market' is in term of a place. For example the Columbus, Ohio market.

Good marketers want information to help them interpret past performance as well as plan future activities. Marketers need timely, accurate and actionable information on consumers, competitors and their branded products. It is foremost necessary to make practical decisions for optimum selling output. Through market research marketing managers could understand possible threat and opportunities of his products and make an action plan accordingly.

Marketing research in the field of pharmaceutics is more important and significant in the competitive pharmaceutical marketing and complex nature of patient's problems. Due to advancement of novel drug delivery system, everyday newer drugs are discovering to facilitate the customer. For this marketing research is not limited to large pharmaceutical companies with big budget but smaller companies is often carrying out this research activities by everyone in the company and by customers too.

Market Research: Market research can be defined as the systematic design, collection, and analysis and reporting of a data and relevant facts to a specific marketing situation facing the company. A company can obtained marketing research in a number of ways. Most large companies have their own marketing research departments, whichoften play crucial roles within the organization.

Market Research Categories

They fall into six categories:

- **Syndicated-service research firms:** These firms gather information from consumer and traders which they sell for fees. Ex: Nielsen media research.
- **Custom marketing research firms:** These firms are hired to carry out specific projects. They design the study and report the findings.
- **Specialty-line marketing research firms:** These firms provide specialized research services. The best example in the pharmaceutical field is service firms, which sells field interviewing services to other firms.
- **Professional institutes:** Professors and students are engaged to carry out projects in collaboration with the different companies.
- **Using the internet:** A company can collect considerable information at very little cost by examining competitor's websites, monitoring chart rooms accessing published data.
- **Checking out rivals:** Many small companies routinely visit their competitors. Firms are jointly do some research work for better of their existingproducts. By this way, cost involvement will be shared by all the companies, reduce the research cost.

Research Process: It involves six steps as below:

(a) Define the problem and objectives.

(b) Develop the research plan.

(c) Collect the information.

(d) Analyze the information.

(e) Present the finding.

(f) Make the decision.

Define the problems and objectives: Problems are defined carefully avoiding too large or too small elaboration. Simultaneously the marketing researchers must set specific research objectives

(a) What types of dosage form to be prepared solid, semisolid or liquid.

(b) What types of patients to be targeted.

(c) How much cost to be involved.

(d) Expected return.

Develop the research plan: The second stage of marketing research is to develop the most efficient plan for gathering the needed information. At the sometime to know the cost of the research plan before approving it. Suppose the company made a prior estimate that launching the liquid suspension of ampicillin, would yield a long-term profit of 50 croresrupees. The manager believes that the doing research would lead to an improved pricing and promotional plan are a long-term profit of 90 crorerupees. In this case, the manager should be willing to opened up to 100 crore rupees on this research. If the research would cost more than 40 crores, it is non worthdoing.Research plan based a data sources, type of approaches, instrumentsinvolves, sampling plan and contact methods.

Collection of information: The data collection place of marketing research is generally the most expensive and the most prone to be error. Information is collected in different way from

(a) Mail questionnaire

(b) Telephone interview

(c) Patient /doctor counseling

(d) Online interview

Before that a sampling plans to be made who is to be surveyed? How many people should be surveyed? How should the responses to be chosen?

Analyze the information: To extract the finding from the collected data the researchers tabulates the data and develops frequency distributions. The researcher will also apply some advanced statistical techniques and decision models in the hope of discovering additional findings.

(i) **Present the finding:** As the last step, the researcher presents the finding. The researcher should present finding that are relevant to the major marketing decisions facing management.

(ii) **Make the decision:** The manager who commissioned the research need to weigh the evidence. If their confidence in the finding is low, they way decide against introducing another alternative process.

(iii) Tools used for marketing research performance: There are four tools are used to check on plan performance.

(a) Sales analysis

(b) Market share analysis

(c) Marketing expense to sales analysis

(d) Financial analysis

Sales analysis: It consists of measuring and evaluating actual sales in relation to goals. Two specific tools are used in sales analysis

(a) Sales variance analysis

(b) Micro sales analysis

Sales variance analysis: It measures the relative contribution of different factors to a gap in sales performance.

Micro salesanalysis: It looks at specific products, territories and so forth that failed to produce expected sales. Suppose the company sells in three territories and expected sales were 1500 units,500 units and 2000 units respectively. The actual sales volume was 1400 units, 525 units and 1075 units respectively. Thus territory one showed a 7 percent shortfall in terms of expected sales; territory two a 5 percent improvement over expectation and territory three a 46 percent shortfall. Then the territory three is causing most of the trouble. So sales vice president needs to check into territory three. May be territory three sales representative is under performing; a major competitor has entered this territory or business is in a recession in this territory.

Market share analysis: Company sales do not reveal how well the company is performing relative to competitor's. For this management needs to track its market share. Conclusion from market share analysis is subject to certain qualifications.

(i) The assumption that outside forces affect all companies in same way is often not true.

(ii) The assumption that a company's performance should be judged against the average performance of all companies is not always valid.

(iii) Sometimes a market share decline is deliberately engineered to improve profits.

(iv) Market share can fluctuate for many minor reasons.

Marketing expense to sales analysis: Annual plan control requires making sure that the company is not overspending to achieve sales goals. The key ratio towards is market expense to sales ratios. It includes

- Sales force to sales
- Advertising to sales
- Sales promotion to sales
- Sales administration to sale percentage.

Financial Analysis: Management uses financial analysis to identify the factors that affect the company's rate of return on net worth. The return on net worth is the product of two ratios, the company's return on assetsanalysis's financial average. It also includes profit analysis.

Application of marketing research: Market research helps to measure and forecast the size, growth and profit potential of each market opportunity. Company can prepare as many as 90 different types of demand estimates. Demand cause measured for six different levels, five different space levels and three different time levels. A company might forecast short run demand for a particular product for the purpose of ordering raw materials, planning production and borrowing cash. It might forecast regional demand for its major product line to decide whether to set up regional distribution.

Market demand for a product is the total volume that would be brought by a defined customer group in a defined geographical area in a defined time period in a defined marketing environment under a defined marketing program. It is not fixed number.

UNIT 1

CHAPTER 1

MARKETING

1.1 General Concept

In the early twentieth century pharmaceutical industry was not well recognized as a complete market like other industries.At the same time there were no antibiotic,no corticoids,only a few sulfa drugs,a few vitamins,no tranquilizers,no anti-hypertensive, noantihistaminic,no tranquillizer,no oral contraceptive drugs, no effective oral diabetic drugs,no prophylactic for gout, no potent active oral diuretics, no drugsto lower the level of blood lipid and cholesterol in plasma,and no vaccines against polio,measles or mumps.

Now a day every one recognized this pharmaceutical market as a self and well developed field of marketing system in making these drugs available at the right time, at the right place, in the right quantity, at a reasonable price and with right information. Pharmaceutical marketing is now specialized that pharmacist involved in the area exclusively for either pharmaceutical dosage forms or for diagnostics kits or for medical devices. Again it is also specialized either general medicines or for antihypertensive or for antibiotics etc for health care items.

1.1.1 Marketing and Pharmaceutical marketing:

A common use of the term '**market**'is in term of a place where exchange of items with moneytakes place. For example the Columbus,where market for Over-The – Counter (OTC) drugs refers to a specific geographic area in which the exchange of drugs takes place. Any success of business organization depends on marketing ability and makes profit. A market must understand what marketing is, how it works, what is marketed and who will market the items.

What is marketing?

Marketing is about identifying and meeting human and social needs. Traditionally it can be defined as marketing is an organizational function and a set of processes for creating, communicating, processing and timely delivering items to customers which gives benefit to the organization. Pharmaceutical marketing involves two step processes first meets the needs of the patients, because patients have no knowledge about the result or effect of the application of medicines or drugs. So pharmaceutical marketing is professional based and pharmaceutical industries take challenging role in selling the pharmaceutical goods.

What are the objects to be marketed?

There are various entities to be marketed such as goods, service, events, properties, ideas and information. Information is essentially what medicines, who, where and which companyproduce,marketand distribute at a priceto the patients. The production,packaging,storing anddistribution of information are prime important activities of the pharmaceutical organizations. Even the companies that sell physical products attempt to add value through the use of information. For example the chief executive officer of a medical business house can say 'our business is utilizing health care information technology and our end product is really say electronic patient record, information on lab tests, pathology and drugs as well as voice dictation.

Pharmaceutical products are broadly classified in two groups on the basis of marketing. These are ethical products and over-the counter products. The ethical products are promoted through the Medical Representatives (M.R) as well as Professional Sales Representative(PSR).Its market depends on the prescription of the physician through the patients.OTC products are promoted by direct advertisement and the patient can purchase directly from the shop without prescription.

Who markets?

A marketer is someone who seeks a response-attention andpurchase from one party called the prospect.Pharmaceutical products are sold by doctors as on need of the patient. It is a needbased demand. Consumer purchases vary on a seasonal, monthly, weekly, daily or even hourly basis or as per doctor's advice. In proactive marketing follows a logical process. The process consists of analyzing marketing opportunities, selecting targeted markets, designing marketing strategies, developing marketing program and managing the marketing effort. In highly competitive market places, planning is more fluid be moving forward with marketing programs involving products and services, staying in touches with customer needs and seeking new advantages rather than relying on present strength.Today's market place is fundamentally different as a result of major societal forces that have resulted in new consumers and companies capabilities. These forces have created new opportunity and challenges. Marketing management has changed significantly in recent years as companies seek new ways to achieve marketing excellence. The success of a marketing management depends on how they develop strategy and plans, capturing marketing insights, connecting with customers, building brands, shaping market offerings, delivering and communicable value and creating long term growth.

Pharmaceutical marketing: Marketers must have derived quantitative and qualitative skills and a keen understanding of how marketing can create value within their organization. They must work in harmony with sales function. Pharmaceutical marketing is based on five key areas:

(i) Strengthening the brand, improved brand value.
(ii) Measuring marketing effectiveness.
(iii) Driving new product development based on patient's needs.
(iv) Gathering information from the patients from market survey.
(v) Utilizing new marketing technology like novel drug delivery systems.

There are a few factors that enabled Indian Pharmaceutical companies to enter into the global market.One such factor is the availability of skilled man-power including a pool of scientists,technicians and pharmacists. Pharmaceutical companies leveraged this advantages as the man-power within the country was considerable cheap compared to those in the developed countries. Another factor that especially helped the India manufactured was to tie-up with foreign companies and enjoyed a free region in domestic market for long. The change in the Intellectual property right (IPR) regime has affected the domestic Pharmaceutical sector adversely. The change over from the process patent regime to the product patent regime affects the industry in a big way. Over the years, the portfolio of drugs exported from India has expanded and so has the scientific talent pool and expertise in formulation and synthesis capabilities. These capabilities helped Indian pharmaceutical companies go far the global market.

Companies that do not have R&D section, they can formulate and market the new products through contractual manufacturing route. This enables the domestic companies to expand their business globally. The world health organization estimates a short fall of over 12.9 million health workers including medical professionals by the year 2035, while 1/3 rd of the world's population lack access to essential medicines.

A key factor to attain and accelerate progress on universal health coverage is the development of human resources, particularly in health supply chains. Personnel involved in health supply chains need to be trained, retained and sufficiently resourced so that the health commodities reach the last mile to the end consumer in need. Efficient supply chains are vital in ensuring beneficiaries receive the health products they need.Workforce development is currently the most important aspect in the field of pharmaceutical marketing for delivering the right kind of drugs in right time with minimum inventory cost. Thepresence of adequately qualified personnel will increase proper utilizations of drugs through doctor, pharmacist interaction and understanding.

Most developing countries do not have dedicated personnel for supply chain function for supplying in a health facilities are managed by pharmacist and nurses.

The Pharmaceutical industry in India ranks 3rd in the worldin terms of volume and 13th in terms of value according to department ofPharmaceuticals, ministry of chemicals and fertilizers. Government started to encourage the growth of drug manufacturing by Indian companies in early 1960 and with the patent act in 1970. Every year Indian Pharmaceutical growth clocked around 17%. Today India has gained immense importance and covered a self sufficient in the domestic market. For exampleIt may be anything like formulation, bulk drug, generic,novel drug delivery system. Size of the industry covers 70% of country's domen for bulk drug, drug inter mediatory, formulations, tables, capsule, orals and injectables.In India there are approximately 250 numbers of large industries and about 8000 numbers of small industries. Theunitsprocedure have the complete ranges of medicine which are ready for consumption by patents.The products are medical devices, diagnostic kits. OTC,bio-chemicals pharmaceuticals.

Green marketing: Now-a-days consumers have to play an important role if companies pay more responsible for preserving the environment during production of a product. There are two ways for controlling the environments-one by improving the processes of formulation. Example: tablet coatings done by using aqueous solvent instead of organic solvent coating.

Secondly by developing the technology using environment friendly machineries. Example:Rapid mixing granulator is used for granulation where all the operations of granulation is done by in a single machine and in a closed system to minimize the expose to the working area.

Consumers stop buying products of companies which are polluting the environment. They are willing to pay an extra amount if a company is incurring extra cost in makingtheproduct with environment friendly processes.They have to understand thatif the companies have to bear all the cost of preserving the environment they will find ways to comply with laws. In pharmaceutical companies follow the Good Manufacturing Practices led down by drug controlled of India In form of schedule M. Manufacturer must know there is no man made resources from which they can get those for preparation of products. We are not anywhere making our own air and water. Companies are always finding out the processes to create confidence of the customersby showing the environment processes applied during manufacturing on the label of the product.

1.2 Scope of marketing

Marketing is performed within a certain environment which itself is always changing. With this changed environment, marketing activities have to change to make this process continuously effective. Marketing activities are divided into four basic elements which are together referred to as the marketing MIX. These are i) product ii) price iii) promotion iv) place. The first 'P' of this 4Ps of marketing MIX is known as goods or services by the organization. Once the needs are identified, it is necessary to prepare the product through product development strategies.Marginal or non-profitable products should be removed unless they are contributing in some way to the overall benefit of the organization. For marketing the pharmaceutical products one should understand the importance of various component of marketing MIX.

Product is the useable item produced from a firm/ industry. It includes processed item (tablet,capsule,cream etc), packaging components(container,carton,leaflets,appli cator etc).Components shall be such which can provide safety of the item.

Price refers to the money value that the customer has to pay. It involves consideration of the profit margin, the cost of production, the possibility of sales at different prices and the concept of the right price.

Promotionis the aspect of advertising or communicating the benefits of the product/ service to the target customers or market segment involved in order to persuade them to buy such product or services. Sometimes customers survey to be conducted to find out the problem facing by the customers.

Finally **place** or physical distribution refers to the aspect of the channel of distribution through which the product has to move before it reaches the customers. It includes the logistics aspects of distribution, warehousing and transportation.

1.3 Distinction between 'marketing' and 'selling'.

Marketing includes all four characteristics of marketing MIX like:

(a) Product
(b) Price
(c) Promotion
(d) Place

Whereas selling includes all four characteristics of selling MIX like:

(a) Prospecting
(b) Presentation
(c) Closing
(d) Follow up.

Table 1

Steps involve in marketing	**Steps involve in selling**
Creation of demand/Advertisement	Pre-sale preparation
Creation of needs	Prospecting
Distribution	Approaching
Storing/Preservation	Presentation
Transportation	Complaint handling
Product Development/Customer survey	Closing
Selling	Follow up.

1.4 Marketing environment:

Marketing environment based on the type of consumers for whom a sell person wishes to market an item. This can be well elaborated by selling perfumes. Perfumes can be purchased by both man and woman. Suppose you have selected women as your group of customers and removed man from your target group. At the same time you have gone still further in defining your customer target by deciding to aim only at the sophisticated group. Our definite preference group would give us two more channels i) highly income group and ii)in the urbane area .It has following components i) economic ii) political iii) technological iv) cultural v) competitive.

Marketing environment is always influenced by the purchasing capacity of the customers, the economic conditions of country.The high cost cancer drugs are till beyond the reach of the poor people.Butsometimes the political pressures or thepersuade can compromise the price of the product for the benefits of the general people. Sometimes technological development cost of product processing can be lowered keeping the profit margin unchanged. In considering the size of the market, the marketer must study the country's economy, country's industrial structure. Manufacturing begins to account for between 10 and 20 percent of the country's gross national product. The industrialization creates a new rich class and a small but growing middle class or both demanding new types of goods, some of which can be satisfied only by imports. Another important economic characteristic is the country's income distribution. Income distribution is related to a country 'industrial structure but is also affected by the political system. The international marketer distinguished countries with five different income distribution patterns-i)very low income ii) mostly low income iii) very high income iv) low, medium, high income and v) mostly medium income.

Political stability is another issue. Government change hands mean change in business policies. Price of the raw materials and finished goods go up and down according to the new government's change inn policies like implement of GST (goods and service tax)

1.5 Good Marketing Policies (GMP):

The product or service which will be marketed must be unique with respect to its quality, adequate to easily applicableandsatisfy the customer's need. During pricing the product, the product has to be adequately priced that customer can pay. This also provide profit margin. The benefits of the product or service can be communicated easily through various ways of advertising and through collective sales promotion. It also concerned with all time availability to their nearest stock holders. This concerned with selection of distribution channels. The organizations must decide whether it should sell through wholesales and then to retailers or whether directly to the consumers. There are many ways in which a product can be moved from producer to the consumer. The optimum method has to be determined in terms of both consumer satisfaction and profitable to the organization. The main objective of GMP is to provide the right type of product like solid /liquid / semi-solid dosage form as per the requirement of the patient at right time when physician prescribe at right price patient's affordability.

1.6 Consumer buying behavior:

Purchase of consumable goods is done by individual or by group. Each person may assume a role in the decision making process. The person who starts the process of considering a purchase is the inicitor,since he feels the need for the product. He sometimes influences other customer to purchase the item. In this regard teenager may consider his friends.The payer is the individual; wit the power and financial authority to purchase the product. The payer is usually persuaded to have a large influencing power on th product. Purchase as the spending power lies with him.

Sometimes form a society and purchase their requirements in bulk from the whole sealers at whole sale rates and sell them to their members at the market rate. The capital requirement for running such store is subscribed by members of such societies. Thus even poor consumers can become member of such society. These stores are usually managed by honorary member but sometimes sale manager may be appointed. By this way a consumer gets better quality goods at lower price. It increases the customers's economic security. The overhead expenses are reduced because unnecessary expenditure on advertisement and decoration of store is not required. The advantage is these stores cannot run on a large scale. Purchasing is done by individuals or by groups such as household goods. Machines are purchased by team members of a purchasing department. When a team or a group may interact to influence the purchase decision. Each person may assume a role in decision making process. The person who starts the process of considering a purchase is the initiator,since he feels the need for the product. He may also initiate the search for information about the purchase decision on his own or by involving others.For example, a teenager may act as an initiator for a mobile set that he wants for commuting, a patient need medicine for his ill health.In these cases the influencers attempt to persuade others in the decision making process to influence the outcome of the decision making process. The decider is the person who makes the ultimate choice regarding product to buy. Buyer conducts the transaction. He visits stores, makes payments and effectdelivery. Usually the buyer is the only player whom the marketer can see being involved in the decision making process. Sometimes the user may or may not be the initiator. Somepoints to be noted in the decision making process for consumers.

(i) Intensity of involvement of purchasing depends on cash value of items. In case of low cost product such as pen where role of buyer is negligible, but in high cost item there is a clear separation of buyer role.

(ii) Again product type determines intensity of buyer's involvement. Women's role has been found to be stronger for house-hold products. Respective roles may change according to product categories. Joint decision making is more common when a house hold consists of two earning members.

(iii) Teenagers play an important role in purchasing high technology products. Their role is greater as influencers than as spenders. High costs products usually involve more people in decision making process as risk associated with the purchase decision are high.

(iv) For medicinal products excerpter influence and emotional influence are used by members to sway other members. It is also important to identify the criteria used by the influencer and deciders to make decision.

Need recognition
↓
information search
↓
evaluation of alternatives
↓
Purchase
↓
Post purchase evaluation

1.7 Industrial buying behavior:

In this form of business the buyers get credit from the seller against the security of a lien on the goods purchased by them. The buyer may not to pay whole amount at a time. The buyer only pay a part of the purchase price of goods and the rest of the price is paid in equal periodical installments (i.e. monthly, half-yearly or yearly).The ownership of the goods continues to be with the seller and transferred to buyer only when he has paid the final installment of the price of goods. In case of default, the seller is forced to take back the goods from the buyer.Under the high hire-purchase system, the sales does ot take place until the last installment for the goods has been paid. These installments always include interest as seller has to want for sometimes till the full price is received. The system provides facilities to purchase costly goods, such as refrigerator, TV set, car, scooter etc.The system helps to increase the sale of the costly and non-essential luxury articles,because it tempts a very large number of peoples to buy the same. Among the various disadvantages one important is people may be tempted by installment plans to buy this which they cannot afford at a time.

For industrial buying dealers play a key role in decision making process. This is because the consumer (here purchase manager) knows only the brand names of items and its application. The purchase manager does not know which brand is more effective for their work.The dealers can supply necessary information about its effectiveness. For an industry an advertisement may stimulate search for more information regarding the advertised product and also may stimulate information search about rival brand. The screening process to narrow down the choice to a few brands may use different choice criteria before making the final choice.

(i) For high involvement purchases typically incur high expenditure or personal risk. The industry people spend more time and effort in arriving at the 'right' decision.

(ii) For low involvement products incur less expenditure and less personal risk and hence the consumer spends less time effort in such decisions.

Case Study 1

Creating a marketer athlete will entail putting him through tough paces early in his career. Easy and early success may make him take success granted.

The marketing manager should have developed a knack for spotting the spark in a young and prospective marketer through his dealing with other marketers in the past. If his academic, behavioral and attitudinal credentials are reasonable, the manager should take him under his wings. Right in the beginning it is important to find out what protégé does best and what he can do best. He should be assigned tasks that he does not particularly like doing, so that he does not develop distaste for any particular activity early in this career. He should be asked to do things that he would not even dream of. He is drilled. The marketing manager treats his protégé with tough love. But the marketer should take care not to hurt his ego, as the bad experiences that happen in training program seem to have a way of sticking around lot more than good things. The young marketer should not end up having a bruised ego. He is sensitive and the manager should never take the tryout of him. If he loses the try ,the joy of participating and competing , he will not perform to his potential. The young marketer should come through the ranks. The prestigious projects can wait. He should not be spoiled by earning big laurels early in his career. But the manager needs to find assignments where he can gain his confidence. After achieving a few success and failures the young marketer can train his gun on the big goose.

Case Study 2

Making of an effective marketer entails a disciplined approach of identifying marketing tasks and carrying them out diligently.

Successful marketers come in all shapes and sizes. There is no particular personality trait which is common to all of them but all successful marketers have followed some common practices. These practices look deceptively simple, and some marketers may fool themselves into believing that they are already practicing them. But most of them will not be, and introspection would not be such a bad idea for them. Fanciful as this discipline into its cadres, as this is all it will take to inculcate these practices into the marketers. The first practice is to find out what marketing teams needs to do. The marketers would have some plans. He would like to strengthen the brand, go global and so on. But the more pertinent question is to find out what needs to done rather than what the marketer would like to do. The distribution system of the company may be in complete disarray and may need immediate fixing. The marketer should prioritize the tasks that need to be done and focus on one or two of them, and not fixing. The marketer should prioritize the tasks that need to be done and focus on one or two of them, and not more, as his limited time and attention would be too thinly spread. After the particular task is complete, he should not move on to the next urgent in the list but create a new list of task and their priorities. He should again focus on the most urgent task in the new list. For instance, after fixing the distribution system, he does not move on to hire a new advertising agency which was the next important task in the original list but makes a new list and finds that an impending product launch is the most important task that the marketing team has to handle. So he has to focus on the launching the product now.

The marketers also need to determine the tasks which need his personal attention and those which can be delegated to competent subordinates. He focuses his attention on the former. For instance he may have determined that the product launch can be handled by a competent subordinate and does not require his direct involvement. So he lets the subordinate handle the product launch and he himself concentrates on strengthening the brand which was the next important task on the list and which he feels requires his direct involvement.

The next important practice is to find out what is good for the customer and hence for the good company also. This requires some soul searching. The marketers have to ascertain and be absolutely that customer interests are being served before that of any stakeholder. The marketer is a custodian of customer interests & their spokesperson. The marketer has to ensure that whatever is good for the customer and the organization is done.

The marketer needs to write down a plan of action. That the plan can go haywire should never be an excuse for not writing down a plan of action. The role of the marketer himself his colleagues, people from other departments and outside agencies should be clearly delineated. Various activities that need to carry out should be spelt out, clearly specifying when they would start and when they should end and who would be responsible for having those activities carried out. Considering the uncertainly of markets fickleness of customers, the marketer fixes some check-points. These check-points are some points in time from the start of plan where it would be verified that conditions and assumptions have not changed enough as to alter the plan or modify it and to verify that the plan has achieved its intermediate goals and is on the right track. These check –points provide flexibility to the plan. If situation demands that the plan change its course or some activities are speeded up or some personnel be replaced, they can be done. These are points to pause and to take stock. And finally the plan should mention the type of result expected.

When a good marketer takes a decision, he takes upon himself the responsibility to communicate the decision to everyone who will be effected by it or has a role in its implementation. When a marketer decides to run a sales promotion, he has to inform, salesperson, retailers, production department, advertising agency, transporters and so on. He also lays down conditions and situations under which a decision can be reviewed , and is not averse to reversing a decision if conditions and situations have changed sufficiently. A marketer is always interested in knowing the results of his decisions. The results tell him about his competence in reading, making the right environments, making the right assumptions and allocating right people for right jobs.

The marketer knows that the ways of the customers will change. Markets will change. He is convinced that a change scenario will come with new opportunities and is confident that he will be able to take advantage of those opportunities. The conviction and the confidence is borne out of the fact and he spends considerable time with his lead customers, has his nose in research laboratories and is always nudging his organization to be more innovative.

Like everyone in the organization the marketer spend a good part of his time in meetings. A good marketer calls a meeting for a specific purpose and battles through the distractions to achieve that purpose. The purpose is announced at the beginning of the meeting. It is important to make meetings purposeful, as otherwise participants begin considering them frivolous and an intrusion in their activities and remain switched off even when they are attending one. A good follow up is also essential and finally a good marketer would always be found chanting, "We did it".

Case Study 3

Customers are unable to talk about products they have never used, or give entirely new ideas for improving products that they are using. Such ideas have to come from companies.

Customers are inept at providing suggestions about products they have never used. Customers, as most human beings, like to have a point of reference from where they take their thoughts forward. Therefore when suggestions are asked for a product he is using, the customer uses the product as the reference point and is able to offer ideas for modifications, improvement and simplification. But even here he is incapable of suggesting entirely new features, benefits or services. Customer's ideas will always be circumscribed by their own experiences. They are incapable talking about products, services, benefits and features they have not experienced themselves. Therefore researchers will draw a blank when they ask customers about new products which have not been in existence till now. They will also not get bolder ideas about product improvements or modifications. Customers can only suggest simple modifications or improvements about a product that they are using. To get meaningful contributions from customers, companies will have to put some version of the product & their mind will start ticking about giving suggestions for small improvements& modifications in the particular version of the product. Company cannot trust customers to give big ideas. Companies will have to do this job themselves. Customers can just vet their ideas.

Case Study 4

For satisfied customers, observation studies make more sense than survey researches.

In most product categories customers are sufficiently satisfied with the products they are using. When satisfied customers are probed through interviews and questionnaires, useful information does not emerge from them. Whatever needs or requirements could be verbalized by customers are already provided by companied. If does not mean that products are perfect and customers are completely satisfied. But what it means is that dissatisfaction is at the subconscious or habitual level for customers, and it is not bothering them enough to surface and be expressed. Companies will have to observe and understand the context in which the product is being used to able to unearth these dissatisfactions. One way to do this is to station people with very observant minds on locations where the products are being used. These people take note of minute expressions of frustrations & irritations of users and contemplate changes that could be made to the product.

UNIT 1

CHAPTER 2

PHARMACEUTICAL MARKETING

2.1 Introduction to Pharmaceutical Marketing

The American Marketing Association defines marketing is the performance of business activities that directs the flow of goods and services from producer to consumer or user. It is much more selling or advertising although those do form part of the marketing function. Schematically this definition can be reproduced as shown below:

PRODUCER ⟶ COSUMER

Through

Advertisement, Distribution, Warehousing / Storing Transportation Selling

Those include as marketing activities. PhlipKotler, well known author in the area of marketing defines marketing as a human activity directed at satisfying needs and wants through exchange processes. ‹Pharmaceutical marketing is not always based on satisfying the patient's need that is the advisable to the patient for use the medicines. Pharmaceutical sales executives are also given products (medicines and cosmetics) and asked to sell them. Therefore to them marketing often starts with the production of a pharmaceutical new product.

Modern concept of marketing is to identify the needs which require satisfaction among human beings. Once the needs of a group of human beings are identified, accordingly generation of a product is made and simultaneously supplies the product to that segment of human being. Now-a-days marketing is often considered the more important function as compared to production. Products are designed and developed by inventors who hoped that they would be sold. If these products fail to satisfy some needs, they would never sell in the market place. Therefore consumer oriented thinking become necessary for any business for survival and growth.

Peter Drucker stresses that marketing is so important that it is not enough to have a strong sales department entrusted with marketing. In his view 'concern and responsibility for the marketing must permeate all areas of the enterprises'. Normally a sales man would like to think of his activities as selling processes. He is more concerned with handling over his product and receiving money in exchange. This would be effective until unless he will start feeling and thinking on both the services he is offering.

2.2 Quantitative and Qualitative Aspect

The global generic pharmaceutical market worth over150 billion dollar in 2013, growing duringn2013 – 2018. India and China are two country holding huge generic markets in production volume. Over the next five years India achiened15 % to 20% growth.

Growth Analysis: The patent expiry of several key antipsychotics and anti-depressants contribute to the rapid growth of CNS drugs market between 2010 and 2017. Development of Fast Growing, reason behind such enormous growth is the massive number of patent expiries. Almost half of the global asthma and COPD market drugs are set to lose patent protection by 2016. Development/ Fast Growing Fast Growing. One of the promising segments for generic participants to venture between 2010 and 2015 is oncology as drugs worth $10 b are set to lose patent protection by 2015.14% CNS Oncology Bubble size represents market value Rheumatology Declining. Decline due to promotion of branded drugs and new innovative formulations such as inhalable insulin are all likely to deter the growth of generics. 2% Cardiovascular relatively lesser number of drugs are subjected to generic exposure during the forecast period and hence the decline in growth. Respiratory Diabetes Dermatology Genitourinary Others Source: Frost & Sullivan analysis.

Mergers & Acquisitions Outlook Generic Pharmaceutical Market: Number of Deals and Amount Spent on Mergers and Acquisitions Globally between 2000 – 2009. The number of deals and the total expenditure on mergers and acquisitions have been increasing steadily over the years since 2000.The trend is likely to continue with all the key generic participants increasing their dependence on strategic alliances to conquer market shares. Source: Thomson Reuters and Frost & Sullivan analysis.

Competitive Landscape Analysis Generic Pharmaceutical Market: Ranking of Top Five Companies by Market Share (Global) Rank company. The top three companies namely Teva, Sandoz and Mylan registered significant growth rates of 16, 14 and 11% respectively in 2010 - 2011.Most of the big companies prefer mergers and acquisitions to organic growth as a faster means to consolidate and expand their market shares. The top five generic pharmaceutical companies accounted for 40% of the share in the global generic pharmaceutical market.

2.3 Size and composition

The Indian Pharmaceutical Market (IPM) accounts for approx. 3% of the global pharmaceutical industry in value terms and 20% in the volume terms. Indian pharmaceutical market is the world's largest supplier of generic drugs, accounting for 20% of global export volume. The growth in 2018 stood at 10% over the same period last year. Owing to robust historical growth, many MNC companies have active presence in the Indian pharmaceutical space.

Besides the domestic market, Indian pharmaceutical companies also have a large chunk of their revenues coming from exports. Major companies have revenues coming in from the sale of intermediates, active pharmaceutical ingredients (APIs), and formulations in various global markets. These include developed markets like US, Europe and Japan and semi developed markets across the world. Markets., Some companies also derive revenues by providing custom research and manufacturing services to innovator companies. Biopharmaceuticals is also increasingly becoming an area of interest given the complexity in manufacture and limited competition.

2.4 Demographic Description

There are ways to target a specific market for your product or service. Demographic segmentation is one of the ways to target a specific group of consumers. Read on to learn more about demographic segmentation and its advantages and disadvantages.

Demographic segmentation is market segmentation according to age, race, religion, gender, family size, ethnicity, income, and education. Demographics can be segmented into several markets to help an organization target its consumers more accurately. With this type of segmentation, an organization can categorize the needs of consumers.

Advantages of Demographic Segmentation

One of the main advantages of demographic segmentation is that the information you need is readily available for you. You can pull census data to determine who, where, and how you want to market your product. For example, automobile industries can market their cars to different age

Another way that businesses, such as automobile industries, don't miss out on the growing market is by providing employees who are bilingual to work with their customers. It is now very common to see business, TV, and newspapers in Spanish as well as English.

Another advantage of demographic segmentation is customer retention and loyalty. When an organization spends time focusing on its customers and their wants and needs, customers will typically come back for repeat business. In our automobile industry example, customers will come back or recommend their friends and family if they were satisfied with their purchase.

2.5 Socio-psychological characteristic of market

Who, exactly, is a consumer? Before we understand the psychological factors driving consumers' buying behavior, it is important that we understand who consumers are. Consumers can be a single consumer, or a consumer can be an organization. Consumers can be any legal person that's buying goods and services from you. These are economic goods and services, and are typically paid for with a widely recognized currency. Typically, the consumer is also the end user or end target of the goods and service a business produces. There are three main definitions for a consumer. You can define a consumer singly or as a combination of these definitions.

A consumer is an organization or an individual targeted by a company to sell their services or product to.

A consumer is an organization or an individual that pays a price to use the services or products that are produced by your organization.

A consumer is an organization or an individual who is the final user of the services or products of a company or organization.

Whether or not to buy a product they come across at a store.

Whether or not to be influenced by marketing campaigns and advertisements for the products and services of a company. It's important to note that marketers get better every day at persuading consumers to buy their products, often without consumers' active awareness that they are being influenced, because advertisers and marketers have a better understanding of the psychological influences in marketing.

What to buy and when to buy it.

Which competitor, among several competitors, to buy from.

The power to make decisions is the central power that is given to a consumer. In fact, everyone has been a consumer at some point in their lives. The main determinant of the consumer market is that everyone has the right, as well as the power, to choose how, when, why, on what, and where to spend their money. Even something as simple as buying a plate of French fries makes you a member of the consumer market because you will pay a certain sum in exchange for the French fries. You are making a decision. You decide to part with some of your hard-earned cash in exchange for a plate of French fries. You also decided to buy from a specific vendor and not a different one. In effect, you choose between competitors. The more active the consumers of an economy are, the more active the economy will be in general.

2.6 Motivation

Happiness is a life devoid of pain and sorrow and filled with intimate life enhancing moments. Our relentless efforts to achieve certain meaningful goals perhaps make us unhappy and miserable. It is our constant quest to eliminate or to ignore the negative like insecurities, failure, sadness and most importantly boredom that causes us to feel anxious or unhappy.

The burden to feel happy is enormous.As if we can buy it or as if we have a right to feel happyregardless.TV and media disseminate a form of propaganda by insisting on and showcasing shiny creative, fulfilling lives. It makes some of us feel inadequate. It is life something good, sometimes bad and often mixture of both.

Maslow of motivation theory: The five-stage model can be divided into deficiency needs and growth needs. The first four levels are often referred to as deficiency needs (*D-needs*), and the top level is known as growth or being needs (*B-needs*).

Deficiency needs arise due to deprivation and are said to motivate people when they are unmet. Also, the motivation to fulfill such needs will become stronger the longer the duration they are denied. For example, the longer a person goes without food, the hungrier they will become.

Maslow (1943) initially stated that individuals must satisfy lower level deficit needs before progressing on to meet higher level growth needs. However, he later clarified that satisfaction of a needs is not an "all-or-none" phenomenon, admitting that his earlier statements may have given "the false impression that a need must be satisfied 100 percent before the next need emerges".

When a deficit need has been 'more or less' satisfied it will go away, and our activities become habitually directed towards meeting the next set of needs that we have yet to satisfy. These then become our salient needs. However, growth needs continue to be felt and may even become stronger once they have been engaged.

Growth needs do not stem from a lack of something, but rather from a desire to grow as a person. Once this growth needs have been reasonably satisfied, one may be able to reach the highest level called self-actualization.

Every person is capable and has the desire to move up the hierarchy toward a level of self-actualization. Unfortunately, progress is often disrupted by a failure to meet lower level needs. Life experiences, including divorce and loss of a job, may cause an individual to fluctuate between levels of the hierarchy.

Therefore, not everyone will move through the hierarchy in a uni-directional manner but may move back and forth between the different types of needs.

2.7 Prescribing habit of a physician:

A medicine is an item which is capable of satisfying the doctor's need.Pharmaceutical industry develops their products into branded which help to create a unique position in the minds of physicians. Brands help physicians distinguished between medicines from different companies in the same kind of drug. Brand superiority leads to high sales, ability to change price premium and power to resist distribution power.

Presently multi products (same characteristics) are available in Indian pharmaceutical market. Doctors normally prescribe the product of big pharmaceutical companies vas they have the concept of that big multinational companies has good manufacturing system as well as they used best quality raw materials. The product produced by them associate with company's prestige, economy. To change their prescription habit, other companies must show such a branded product which has added advantages over existing.

General practitioners and specialists vary substantially in their prescribing habits. In short, the drug selection process is not always rational. What influences the decisions made by clinicians are:

(i) Patient's condition treatable.

(ii) Patient's suitability for treatment.

(ii) Availability of effective and safe medications.

(vi) In many circumstances, physicians recommend treatment even if symptoms are mild.

The doctor's selection is not entirely objective; it is not based solely on scientific facts. It should, however, be reassuring to patients that the most commonly prescribed medications for a given disease or condition have more similarities than dissimilar.

2.7.1 Pescribing Process

Consultation is a fundamental part of prescribing process and prescribers need to understand and utilize this to help them practice effectively. The medical model of disease, diagnosis and prescribing is often center to practice, but an understanding of patient's background together with his or her medical beliefs and anxieties is equally impo5tant in helping the prescriber understand his/her own role and behavior alongside those of his/her patients. A broad range of practical skills are needed in this consultation The steps are a) Interpersonal skills b) reasoning skills c) practical skills.

In addition to those there in need of building the patient-physician relationship.

Building relationship: Nonverbal communication is important and can be used by the prescriber to gain information for the patient. Facial expressions and body posture can give clues about how the patient is feeling.

Providing structure: Providing structure is important in the patient prescriber consultation to enable five keys steps (i) initiating session (ii)gathering information (iii)physical examination (iv)explanation and planning (v)closing session.to be effective completion. Therefore as the power in consultation is with the prescriber. It is the prescriber's responsibility to guide the consultation and involve the patient.

What is the patient's role?

Patients should participate in the decision to treat. They need to know as much as possible about a medication's benefits and potential adverse reactions. Patients need to understand how to take the medication, what the dose is, how long to take the medication, and what they need to do if they suspect that the medication is causing unwanted reactions. It is also important for the treating physician to convey the importance of taking the medication as prescribed, since the suggested treatment regimen often yields the desired outcome. Encouraging patients to follow the prescribed treatment, however, must be tempered with realistic expectations. No guarantees can be given. Nonetheless, an informed patient is always better off. Unfortunately, many patients leave their clinic visits relatively uninformed and unaware of the importance of complying with the prescribed treatment regimen. A surprising number of patients never even go to the pharmacy to fill their prescriptions! As a patient, you should not hesitate to ask for more information if you feel that your physician has not satisfied your need to be fully informed. This is your right.

Is the cost of medication considered?

The price of a prescribed medication is not often discussed between the physician and the patient, but it should be. One reason is that drug prices aren't well known by all physicians. Patients, on the other hand, may be more interested in knowing how much they have to pay, since medications can be expensive. There are a variety of health plans with different co-payment schedules. Patients seeking to limit the cost of their medications should ask if suitable generic medications are available.

Do external factors influence physicians' treatment decision?

It has been documented that doctors are influenced by their peers, in particular their local opinion leaders. In every community there are physicians who a highly respected by their peers, and these physicians are the opinion leaders. These leaders are often targeted by drug companies for promotional purposes. The pharmaceutical companies have very skillful tactics to "convince" doctors to prescribe their products. Marketing tools range from coffee mugs and pens to "promotional trips" targeting desirable destinations and lucrative consulting agreements. Efforts are underway to restrict excessive marketing of medications to physicians.

2.8 Patient's choice of physician

For the study, researchers surveyed 488 respondents to determine the profile of the modern medical patient. Respondents identified as U.S. residents age 18 years and older who had visited a physician for a standard Overall, patients are generally happy with their physicians and many stay with their physicians for a checkup in the past two years at a medical facility other than a free clinic.

Here are six take ways from the survey.

1. Forty-six percent of respondents reported being "very satisfied" with their current physician, compared to 6 percent of respondents who reported decade or more being "very dissatisfied."
2. Analysis discovered patient satisfaction increased with age. Eighty-two percent of patients over the age of 55 identified as being satisfied with their physicians. The rate dropped to 67 percent among patients ages 18 to 34.
3. More than half (51 percent) of respondents said finding an in-network physician was "critical" in their selection process.
4. Researchers also discovered apart from a physician's age, which respondents linked with a physician's experience, those surveyed were largely unconcerned with their physician's demographic profile. However, 23 percent of women strongly preferred having a physician of the same gender, compared to 9 percent of men.
5. Researchers discovered that in addition to cost and experience, respondents also look for a physician that demonstrates competence and a positive attitude.
6. While more than half of physicians surveyed (59 percent) said they wish they had more time to communicate with patients, only 33 percent of patients indicated they wanted more communication time

Demographic Characteristics of Consumer Markets

Characteristics of consumer markets based on demographics include differences in gender, age, ethnic background, income, occupation, education, household size, religion, generation, nationality and even social class. Most of these demographic categories are further defined by a certain range. For example, companies may identify the age of their consumers in the 18 to 24, 25 to 34, 35 to 54, 55 to 65, and 65+ age groups. Companies often identify these demographic characteristics through market research surveys used to discover which demographic groups comprise the majority of their customer base. Companies can then target their advertising towards these demographic groups. For example, a new cell phone may be targeted toward 18 to 24-year-olds with incomes between $25,000 and $50,0

Does it effect organizations and the overall economy? Why is it so important?

Consumer behavior is, for the most part, a psychological process and the psychology of buying behavior is deeply related to the emotions that the consumer goes through. First, the consumer will begin by recognizing the fact that they are in need of the product. They will then find some way to solve their needs. They will find out where they can get the product, how much it costs, which vendors are the best to buy it from, when is the best time to buy it, and so on. Once the consumer is satisfied with all the information they have gathered on the matter, they will implement the plan and make a purchase of the product.

Of course, the process is outlined rather mechanically which gives the implication that consumers approach their buying decisions with a certain academic air and take a lot of time to make the decisions. They do not. In fact, most buying decisions are made in an instant because a lot of the things that consumers buy are neither so expensive nor so important that they need such a detailed thinking process before their purchase is considered. However, for the few things people buy that are expensive and important enough, such as a house, a car, or even an engagement risk, the actual process that they go through before they make the decision is quite similar to the one outlined

2.9 Analyzing the market

Role of market research: Market Research is the pre-requisite for having the knowledge about customers and other aspects of the market environment that effect the company's operation. Questions like what kind of people buy the company's product, what they value in the product and where they buy from, are important. The company needs to find 'real views of the customer and then only should the company design its marketing limitations. This information is obtained by formal and informal means. Informal means like casual discussion with customers, reports of sales people, observation of competitor activities are inadequate to provide the necessary in-depth market knowledge. A more formal approach like collection of data through questionnaire must be applied to supply information system to managers.

2.9.1 Market Information System (MIS)

MIS is formally gathered, stored, analyzed and distributed to managers in accordance with their informational needs at a regular interval on a planned basis. It comprises four elements like:

(a) Internal continuous data

(b) Internal ad-hoc data

(c) Environmental scanning

(d) Marketing research.

Market research is considered as the immediate solution for providing sufficient data to the marketing managers for necessary action and follow-up. It is concerned with the provision of information about market and reaction of these to various product, price, distribution and promotion actions. Market research contributes heavily to marketing MIX planning. There are two ways of market research-

(i) By external continuous data includes television audience monitoring and consumer panels where household purchases are recorded over time.

(ii) By external ad-hoc data are gathered by means of surveys into specific marketing issues including usages and attitude studies,advertising,product testing etc.

2.9.2 Stages in the marketing research process

The process of market research starts with the identification of a problem. Simultaneously the company also identifies whether the required information can be collected by the internal staff or an external market research agency needs to be commissioned.

Step I-Initial contact: There are realization that a marketing problem requires information to help and find its solution. The marketing department may contact the internal marketing research staff or an out-side agency.A meeting is arranged to discuss the nature of problem and the client's research needs. If the client and its market are new to the agency, some rudimentary exploratory research like a search on the internet is conducted prior to meeting.

Step II-Research brief: At the meeting the client explains the marketing problem and the research objectives. The marketing problem may be to attract new customers to a product and research objectives would be to identify customers who can use the product and to identify the features of the product that appeals to them most.

Step III-Prerequisites for a good research: The research brief should be clear about the marketing problem for which research needs to be done. Additionally the company must also take into consideration diverse perspectives of at least two or more marker research agencies to ascertain the accuracy of their research designs. Terms like market. Market share, competitors should be clearly defined for the purpose of the research.

Step IV-Research proposal: Research proposal defines what the marketing research agency promises to do for its client and how much it will cost.It should be written to avoid misunderstanding. It should be demonstrate an understanding of client's marketing and research problem. It should contain an unambiguous description of research design including survey method,type of sample, sample size,collection and analysis of data,when the report will be produced and how much the research will cost.

Case Study 1

The focus and the amount of investment should be adapted to the dynamics of various stages of the product life cycle.

In the early stage of the product life cycle companies have the greatest potential to invest in developing loyal customers. Early entrants alert customers about the existence of the category, define the category in terms of initial consumer preference, influence consumer choice criteria to some extent by their early offering, allow their product to become he base on which consumers compare offerings of later entrants and build a customer base. In these early stages cumulative marketing investment is a strong determinant of market share and therefore early entrants should make adequate investments.

Many products going through the decline stage of the product life cycle will experience a shrinking market coupled with falling sales and profits. For some companies it will simply be a case of continuing to manufacture a product as long as it is economically viable, but withdrawing it as soon as that's not the case. However, depending on the particular markets involved, some companies may be able to extend the life of their product and continue making a profit, by looking at alternative means of production and new, cheaper markets. Even in the decline stage, a product can still be viable, and the most successful manufacturers are those that focus on effective product life cycle management, allowing them to make the most from the potential of each and every product the company launches.

Case Study 2

The ownership of the brand should convey the personality of its user. The brand must be much more than the sum of the product attributes.

Most customers, as individuals, have their own story to tell. They want to perceive as a certain type of person, be it stylish or an environmentalist. It is not only important to be the type of person one wants to be but it is also important that he be seen and recognized as one. Brands can be of great help in signaling to others "WHO" the brand owner is and what he stands for. Therefore a brand has to be endowed with individualism before it can be help in shaping perceptions about its owners. A brand has to be perceived as being friendly to environment or as the one which is always stylish.

Brands must be more than a sum of product attributes. A narrow focus on attributes will lead to short –lived, easily copied advantages and to shallow customer relationships. Strong brands will have to go beyond providing functional benefits and deliver emotional benefits and help people express themselves. Such brands develop their own personality. The brand builders will have to envision a personality of the brand and the brand building programs should promote and cement that personality over a period of time. The brand should have developed associations with intangibles like perceived innovativeness or reputation for quality or always being stylish. The association with intangibles helps to shape definite image of its user. The personality of the brand and the image of its users should match and reinforce each other.

Such a brand will obviate the necessity of a customer telling his story. The brands in his possession will tell the story instead. The mobile phone and the handbag in her hands and the shirt on his shoulders will tell the world who the customer is.

Case Study 3

The success or failure of line extensions depends on internal organizational factors besides customers and competitors.

Majority of new consumer packaged goods launched are line extensions-products added to an existing product line under an established brand name. Because the line extensions are easier and cheaper to launch than entirely new products, companies want to reach untapped markets with them. But most of the times, the endeavor is unsuccessful. Instead of providing customers with clear new value, a line extension becomes another offering among virtually identical products.

Internal organizational factors, and not competitive pressures or consumer demands account for the launch of many undifferentiated line extensions. Companies that create successful line extensions rotate brand assignments of their product managers. The exposure to new ideas helps them to think creatively. They also use smaller product development teams, encourage managers to take more risks and require more rigorous evidence of probable market success before authorizing a line extension. Instead of rushing into getting a product to a market, these companies go at a more deliberate pace, allowing their designers enough time.

Marketing function is organized along product lines which facilitates greater knowledge of individual product lines. Companies planning to successfully launch product line extensions should look at their marketing organizations and development process to find out whether they can make it.

Case Study 4

High tech products also need to be branded in a commoditized era.

Technically trained managers reject the idea of branding their high-tech products. They believe that market success depends primarily on the price-performance ratio an their sophisticated and experienced customers base their purchase decisions on benchmarking studies and objective performance data. They believe that brands are relevant when purchase decisions are irrational or emotional. This notion is wrong. A successful brand in any business commands premium prices because customers consider it is a promise of receiving certain type and level of value. And value is what buyers employing rational decisions are seeking.

Though customers evaluate the product on rational criteria, the parameters on which such products are evaluated complex in nature. The performances of the offering of the major competitors converge and no player allows a competitor to have an edge in a parameter over any significant period of a time. It is not easy for a customer to decide the best product categorically. Under such situations, branding plays a major role. When no offering is decisively better than the other, the offering which is most well-known will be preferred. Markers of such high-tech products should use the mass-media to convey their messages.

When technologies are changes rapidly, customers are not able to decide the offering which incorporates the latest technologies. Customers dread buying high-tech products which are likely to become obsolete soon. Under such circumstances a strong brand provides an assurance to the customers that the brand will incorporate in itself whatever is latest.

UNIT 2

CHAPTER 3

PRODUCT DICISION

Many people think that a product is a tangibleitem, but product can be more than that a product is anything that can be offered to a market to satisfy a want or need. Products are of various kinds which includes physical goods,services,experiences,events,persons,places,properties,organizations,information and ideas.

3.1 Product Classification

Traditionally products are classified on the basis of characteristics, durability, tangibility and use. Batch product type has an appropriate marketing mix strategy.

Durable goods are tangible goods that normally survive many uses:refrigerators, machine tools and clotthings.Durable products normally require more personal setting and service, command a higher margin and require more seller guarantees.

Non-durable goods are tangible good normally consumed in one or a few uses, like beer and soap. These goods are consumed quickly and purchased frequently.

Services are intangible, inseparable, variable and perishableproducts. They normally require more quality control, supplier credibility and adaptability .Exacts legal advice, appliance repairs.

3.2 Consumer goods classification

Consumable goods usually are purchased frequently, immediately and with a minimum effort. Normally consumers are likely to experience an urge or compelling used to make a purchase.

Shopping goods are goods that the consumer in the process of selection and purchase, compare on basis of suitability/quality, price and style. Examples are furniture, car,branded medicines.

Specialty goods are unique in characteristics or branded for which a sufficient number of buyers are willing to make a special purchasing effort. Examplesare photographic equator, men'ssuit, stereo components laptop.

An sought goods are those the consumer does not know about or does not normally think of buying like smoke detectors. Other examples are life imminence, encyclopedias if needs advertising and personal selling support.

3.3 Industrial goods

Are normally used as raw materials as well as other ingredients. They can be classified interims of how they enter the production process and their relative customers and distinguish them into three groups.

Materials and parts are goods that enter the manufacturers product completely. They are raw materials, manufactured materials and parts.

Capital items are long lasting goods that facilitate developing or managing the finished product. They include two groups-

(a) Installation

(b) Equipment

Installation consist of building are heavy equipment. Installation is major purchase. They are usually bought directly from product.

Equipment comprises portable factory equipment and tools. These types of equipment do not become part of a finished product. They have shorter file than installations but a longer life than operating supplies.

Supplies and business services are short term goods and services that facilitate developing or managing finished product .These are maintenance and repair items and operating supplies. Examples:Lubricant, coal.

3.4 Productmix

A product mix is the set of all products and items a particular seller offer for sale. A product consists of various product lists. In general electrical consumer appliance decision there is product line managers for refrigerators, stoves, washing machines.

Product mix consists of communication and computer products. A company is product mix refers a certain width, length, depth and consistency of the market of the product.

(i) The width of a product mix refers to many different product lines which the company do marketing.

(ii) The depth of a product mix refers to the total number of items in the mix.

(iii) The consistency of the product mix refers to how closely relate the various product lines are in end use, production requires distribution channels and or some other way.

(iv) The depth of a product mix refers to how many variants are offered of each product in the line. The average depth of the product mix can be calculated by averaging the number of variants within the brand groups.

These four product mix dimensions permit the company expenditures business in four ways. It can add new product lines; they identify its product mix. It can increase the length of each product line. It can add more product variants to each product line and its product mix. It is useful to conduct product line analysis.

3.5 Product Portfolio Analysis

A company normally does the business to earn profit besides fulfilling the requirement of the customers. So analysis of business in terms of money comes first. They always do the business with multiple product lines. If any single product does not help to earn profit, other product will help to overcome this loss.

A company operates in various business or markets. Each of its businesses operates in different conditions. The corporate has to realize that the each of its business will earn different amount of profits and will require different amount of investments. The corporate should learn to expect different amounts of profits from its different business and should invest in them depending on their requirements.

On BCG (Boston Consulting Group) matrix the market growth and market share par walls shows there are four segments in the business operations. These segments are classified as-

(a) Stars

(b) Problem children

(c) Cash cows

(d) Dogs

In the BCG (Boston Consulting Group) growth share matrix on vertical axis shown market growth rate and horizontal axis relative market share. It acts a s a proxy for competitive strength.

Stars	Problem children
Cash cows	Dogs

Cash flow is dependent on the box in which a product fall.

Stars are market leaders and earn high revenues but require substantial investments to finance growth and to meet competitive challenges.Stars are market leaders and earn high revenue but require substantial investment to finance growth and to meet competitive challenges. Overall cash flow is therefore likely to be roughly in balance.

Problem children are the products in high growth markets which cause a drain on cash flow as they incur huge marketing expenditure in reaching out to growing number of customers. They also incur costs in setting up new manufacturing units to be able to serve the growing markets.

Cash cows are market leaders in mature, low growth market i.e. investment in new production facilities and marketing is minimum. High market share leads to large revenues and hence, positive flow.

Dogs also operate in low growth market but have low market share and therefore, earn low revenues. Except for some products near the dividing line between cash cows and dogs, most dogs produce low or negative cash flows.

3.6 Promotional Budget

A promotional budget is a specified amount of money setaside to promote the products or beliefs of a business or organization. Promotional budgets are created toanticipate the essential costs associated with growing a business or maintaining a brand name.

3.6.1 Methods of determining the total promotion budget

Firms expend considerable amount on promotional activities. Four methods are employed in determining the budget for promotional expenditure. They are detailed as follows.

3.6.1.1 Affordable method

Many companies employ the affordable method for determining the promotion budget. The promotion budget is set in a manner which the company can afford. This method is a subjective assessment, as it pays little attention to the long-term promotional needs of a service. This method does not consider the role of promotion in sales volume. Employment of affordable method very often results in an uncertain annual budget, making the long-range planning difficult.

3.6.1.2 Percentage of sales method

Under this method, promotion expenditure is determined as a percentage of sales. The advantages of Percentage of sales method is:

(a) First, expenditure on advertising is closely related to the sales. So, the company can easily afford to spend a specified percentage of sale on promotion.

(b) Second, this method facilitates an analysis of the relationship among promotion cost and selling price per unit. Third, this method ensures stability when competitors are also spending the same percentage of sales on promotion.

3.6.1.3 Competitive-parity method

Under this method, advertising expenditure of the firm is equal to the amount spent bycompetitors. This method follows the policy of the competitors in respect of promotion budget. It isbased on the assumption that competitor's expenditure represents the prudence of the industry. Since the promotion budget of one firm is in parity with the competitor, promotion war is avoided. However, this method has certain limitations. There is no assurance that competitors' promotionbudget represents collective wisdom of the industry. Companies vary in reputation, resources, objectives and opportunities. So, the promotion budget appropriate to one firm may not be appropriate to the other.

3.6.1.4 Objective and task method

Under this method the proposed budget based on objectives like plan to export or plans to introduce a new line of products or to introduce the product to a new targeted customers etc. Likewise task force set to meet the target.Under this method, marketers determine promotion. In this case expenditure is variable.

3.7 Packaging

Packaging and storing of health care commodities are vital to ensuring their quality. Product expiration date is based on ideal storage condition with right kinds of packing. Therefore the drugs stored in a drug store must be packed in such a way that they are easily traceable and the label must remain the following information.

(i) Product name
(ii) Composition
(iii) Date of manufacturing
(iv) Storage condition
(v) Application guideline
(vi) Category of drug like schedule 'H' or 'E'.
(vii) Manufacturer name and address
(viii) License No.
(ix) Prices/Physician sample (not for sale).

Containers must be such which will meet the following requirements:

(i) It must be non-reactive with medicament
(ii) It should be transparent so that visual inspection can be possible from out-side
(iii) It should be appropriate in size and shape
(iv) Single unit dose can be withdrawn.
(v) It can be easily discarded after use.

Packaging includes all the activities of designing and producing the container for a product. Packages height includesup to three levels of material. It includes primary packaging and secondary packaging component. Well designed packages can create convenience and promotional value. The package is the buyer's first encounter with the product and is capable of turning the buyer on or off. Many marketers have called packaging a fifth-'P' along with price, product, place and promotion.

3.8 Labeling

Sellers must labels products. The label may be a simple tag attached the product or an elaborately designed graphic that is the part of the package .The label might carry only the brand name or a great deal of information. Even if the seller prefers a simple label, the law may require additional information. Labels perform several functions; first the label identifies the product or brand. It might describe the product uses. It shows how to apply (application), date of manufacturing, expire date and price.

The term 'label' means a display of written, printed, or graphic matter upon the immediate container of any article. It is amendatory under authority of this Act that any word, statement, or other information appearing on the label shall not imports, inspections, and enforcement policies. Office of regulatory affair supports the five FDA product centers by inspecting regulated products and manufacturers, conducting sample analysis on regulated products and reviewing imported products offered for entry into thr United States.

Product portfolio analysis is difficult when there are too many problem children and dogs and not enough stars and cash flows. Enough investments showed be made in cows so that they are able to maintain their market share. One or two problem children should be interested; stars should continue to receive adequate support. The aim should be to build existing stars and build market share of chosen problem children. Dog should be harvested or divested if it is believed that it cannot be resume.

3.9 New product decision

New product decision is based on product strategies of the Ansoff's matrix.

The term 'new product' means any product the composition of which is such among experts qualified by scientific training and experience to evaluate the safety and effectiveness of drugs. As safe and effective for use under the conditions prescribed, recommended, or suggested in the labeling thereof, except that such a product not so recognized shall not be deemed to be a 'new drug'.

Business growth is done by servicing new products in their existing market or existing products in new market or existing product in existing market.

To develop a new product for current market is to gain higher sales. New products are developed for market. This is risky. But if there is strategy between existing and new products, this strategy is likely to work.

3.9.1 Product Positioning

Positioning is the perception or the image that a customers have of the company and its product, it is the customer's believes about the company's product being of say high quality or low price or durable etc.This perception is the stimulus of customer's attitude and behaviour towards company's product. Customer's positive perceptions will derive the business of the company and negative perceptions will sink it.

3.9.2 Positioning a new product concept

It is the function of promotional activities. Its first objectives is to build up brand status and secondly the company always talked about the core character of the brand. Through the brand positioning a company can distinguish its product from its competitor's product. Promotional differentiation arises from unique, valued images created by advertising or superior services provided by sales people. By this company has an opportunity to differentiate itself by making it convenience for customer to buy the product.

3.10 Product life cycle

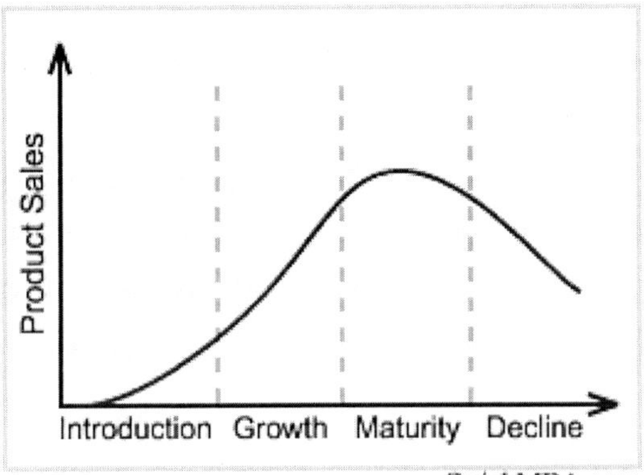

QuickMBA.com

3.10.1 Introduction

The first of the four product life cycle stages is the Introduction Stage. Any business that is launching a new product needs to appreciate that this initial stage could require significant investment. This isn't to say that spending a lot of money at this stage will guarantee the product's success. Any investment in research and new product development has to be weighed up against the likely return from the new product, and an effective improvement plan will need to be developed, in order to give the new product the best chance of achieving this return.

3.10.2 Challenges of the Introduction Stage

(i) **Small or no market:** When a new product is launched, there is typically no market for it, or if a market does exist it is likely to be very small. Naturally this means that sales are going to be low to start off with. There will be occasions where a great new product or fantastic marketing campaign will create such a buzz those sales take off straight away, but these are generally special cases, and it often takes time and effort before most products achieve this kind of momentum

(ii) **High costs:** Very few products are created without some research and development, and once they are created, many manufacturers will need to invest in marketing and promotion in order to achieve the kind of demand that will make their new product a success. Both of these can cost a lot of money, and in the case of some markets these costs could run into many millions of dollars.

(iii) **Losses, Not Profits:** With all the costs of getting a new product to market, most companies will see negative profits for part of the Initial Stage of the product life cycle, although the amount and duration of these negative profits does differ from one market to another. Some manufacturers could start showing a profit quite quickly; while for companies in other sectors it could take years.

3.10.3 Benefits of the Introduction Stage

(i) **Limited competition:** If the product is truly original and a business is the first to manufacture and market it, the lack of direct competition would be a distinct advantage. Being first could help an organization to capture a large market share before other companies start launching competing products, and in some instances can enable a business's brand name to become synonymous with the whole range of products, like Walkman, Biro, Tannoy and Hoover.

(ii) **High Price:** Manufacturers that are launching a new product are often able to charge prices that are significantly above what will eventually become the average market price. This is because early adopters are prepared to pay this higher price to get their hands on the latest products, and it allows the company to recoup some of the costs of developing and launching the product. In some situations however, manufacturers might do the exact opposite and offer relatively low prices, in order to stimulate the demand.

3.10.4. Product Life Cycle Management

The initial stage of the product life cycle is all about building the demand for the product with the consumer, and establishing the market for the product. The key emphasis will be on promoting the new product, as well as making production more cost-effective and developing the right distribution channels to get the product to market.

3.10.5 Growth

The Growth stage is the second of stages in the product life cycle, and for many manufacturers this is the key stage for establishing a product's position in a market, increasing sales, and improving profit margins. This is achieved by the continued development of consumer demand through the use of marketing and promotional activity, combined with the reduction of manufacturing costs. How soon a product moves from the Introduction stage to the Growth stage, and how rapidly sales increase, can vary quite a lot from one market to another.

3.10.6 Challenges of the Growth Stage

(i) **Increasing Competition:** When a company is the first one to introduce a product into the market, they have the benefit of little or no competition. However, when the demand for their product starts to increase, and the company moves into the Growth phase of the product life cycle, they are likely to face increased competition as new manufacturers look to benefit from a new, developing market.

(ii) **Lower Prices:** During the Introduction stage, companies can very often charge early adopters a premium price for a new product. However, in response to the growing number of competitors that are likely to enter the market during the Growth phase, manufacturers may have to lower their prices in order to achieve the desired increase in sales.

(iii) **Different Marketing Approach:** Marketing campaigns during the Introduction stage tend to benefit from all the buzz and hype that surrounds the launch of a new product. But once the product becomes established and is no longer 'new', a more sophisticated marketing approach is likely to be needed in order to make the most of the growth potential of this phase.

3.10.7 Benefits of the Growth Stage

(i) **Costs are reduced:** With new product development and marketing, the Introduction stage is usually the most costly phase of a product's life cycle. In contrast, the Growth stage can be the most profitable part of the whole cycle for a manufacturer. As production increases to meet demand, manufacturers are able to reduce their costs through economies of scale, and established routes to market will also become a lot more efficient.

(ii) **Greater Consumer Awareness:** During the Growth phase more and more consumers will become aware of the new product. This means that the size of the market will start to increase and there will be a greater demand for the product; all of which leads to the relatively sharp increase in sales that is characteristic of the Growth stage.

(iii) **Increase in Profits:** With lower costs and a significant increase in sales, most manufacturers will see an increase in profits during the Growth stage, both in terms of the overall amount of profit they make and the profit margin on each product they sell.

3.10.8 Product Life Cycle Management

The standard Product Life Cycle Curve typically shows that profits are at their highest during the Growth stage. But in order to try and ensure that a product has as long a life as possible, it is often necessary for manufacturers to reinvest some of those profits in marketing and promotional activity during this stage, to help guarantee continued growth and reduce the threat from the competition.

3.10.9 Maturity

After the Introduction and Growth stages, a product passes into the Maturity stage. The third of the product life cycle stages can be quite a challenging time for manufacturers. In the first two stages companies try to establish a market and then grow sales of their product to achieve as large a share of that market as possible. However, during the Maturity stage, the primary focus for most companies will be maintaining their market share in the face of a number of different challenges.

3.10.10 Challenges of the Maturity Stage

(i) **Sales Volumes Peak:** After the steady increase in sales during the Growth stage, the market starts to become saturated as there are fewer new customers. The majority of the consumers who are ever going to purchase the product have already done so.

(ii) **Decreasing Market Share:** Another characteristic of the Maturity stage is the large volume of manufacturers who are all competing for a share of the market. With this stage of the product life cycle often seeing the highest levels of competition, it becomes increasingly challenging for companies to maintain their market share.

(iii) **Profits Start to Decrease:** While this stage may be when the market as a whole makes the most profit, it is often the part of the product life cycle where a lot of manufacturers can start to see their profits decrease. Profits will have to be shared amongst all of the competitors in the market, and with sales likely to peak during this stage, any manufacturer that loses market share, and experiences a fall in sales, is likely to see a subsequent fall in profits. This decrease in profits could be compounded by the falling prices that are often seen when the sheer number of competitors forces some of them to try attracting more customers by competing on price.

3.10.11 Benefits of the Maturity Stage

(i) **Continued Reduction in Costs:** Just as economies of scale in the Growth stage helped to reduce costs, developments in production can lead to more efficient ways to manufacture high volumes of a particular product, helping to lower costs even further.

(ii) **Increased Market Share Through Differentiation:** While the market may reach saturation during the Maturity stage, manufacturers might be able to grow their market share and increase profits in other ways. Through the use of innovative marketing campaigns and by offering more diverse product features, companies can actually improve their market share through differentiation and there are plenty of product life cycle examples of businesses being able to achieve this.

Maturity stage of the product life cycle presents manufacturers with a wide range of challenges. With sales reaching their peak and the market becoming saturated, it can be very difficult for companies to maintain their profits, let alone continue trying to increase them, especially in the face of what is usually fairly intense competition. During this stage, it is organizations that look for innovative ways to make their product more appealing to the consumer that will maintain, and perhaps even increase, their market share.

3.10.12 Decline

The last of the product life cycle stages is the Decline stage, which as you might expect is often the beginning of the end for a product. When you look at the classic product life cycle curve, the Decline stage is very clearly demonstrated by the fall in both sales and profits. Despite the obvious challenges of this decline, there may still be opportunities for manufacturers to continue making a profit from their product.

3.10.13 Challenges of the Decline Stage

(i) **Market in Decline:** During this final phase of the product life cycle, the market for a product will start to decline. Consumers will typically stop buying this product in favour of something newer and better, and there's generally not much a manufacturer will be able to do to prevent this.

(ii) **Falling Sales and Profits:** As a result of the declining market, sales will start to fall, and the overall profit that is available to the manufacturers in the market will start to decrease. One way for companies to slow this fall in sales and profits is to try and increase their market share which, while challenging enough during the Maturity stage of the cycle, can be even harder when a market is in decline.

(iii) **Product Withdrawal:** Ultimately, for a lot of manufacturers it could get to a point where they are no longer making a profit from their product. As there may be no way to reverse this decline, the only option many business will have is to withdraw their product before it starts to lose them money.

3.10.14 Benefits of the Decline Stage

(i) **Cheaper Production:** Even during the Decline stage, there may be opportunities for some companies to continue selling their products at a profit, if they are able to reduce their costs. By looking at alternative manufacturing options, using different techniques, or moving production to another location, a business may be able to extend the profitable life of a product.

(ii) **Cheaper Markets:** For some manufacturers, another way to continue making a profit from a product during the Decline stage may be to look to new, cheaper markets for sales. In the past, the profit potential from these markets may not have justified the investment need to enter them, but companies often see things differently when the only other alternative might be to withdraw a product altogether.

3.10.15 Product Life Cycle Management

Many products going through the decline stage of the product life cycle will experience a shrinking market coupled with falling sales and profits. For some companies it will simply be a case of continuing to manufacture a product as long as it is economically viable, but withdrawing it as soon as that's not the case. However, depending on the particular markets involved, some companies may be able to extend the life of their product and continue making a profit, by looking at alternative means of production and new, cheaper markets. Even in the decline stage, a product can still be viable, and the most successful manufacturers are those that focus on effective product life cycle management, allowing them to make the most from the potential of each and every product the company launches.

3.10.16 Product line portfolios

The process of managing groups of brands and product lines is called portfolio amalysis.The corporate should learn to expect different amounts of profit from its different business and should invest in them depend on their requirements. Under the BCG (Borton consulting group) growth share matrix analysis it has four boxes as given below:

Cash flow is dependent on the bon in which a product falls. Stars are market leaders and earn high revenue but require substantial investment to finance growth and to meet competitive challenges. One in all cash flow is therefore likely to be likely to be roughly in balance.

3.11 Product Management

Product management defines production of right kind of product at right time, at right place, at right price. Naturally Product Management includes production and material handling.

Production is the process by which goods and services are created. A typical production system is shown below:

Decision making

Control

In-put ------------------- Conversion process ------------------- out-put

In-put can be raw materials, components, paper works etc. whereas out-puts are completed parts, products paper-work, services and scraps.

The conversion process involves the receipt and storage of raw materials, means of its transportation(belt, conveyer or pipes).

The out-puts are products, inter mediatory or services.

Product should be developed by means of simplification, standardization, specialization and diversification. It should be acceptable to customers and should satisfy their needs. It should create a good impression on the customers and generate his confidence regarding durability, quality and performance of the product..The design should be such that the product is functionally sound (effective). It should be able to perform the functions for which it is made for, to the complete satisfaction of the consumer. The product design be such that there is sufficient adaptability and scope of improvement in work.

3.11.1 Objectives of product Management

(i) It provides the better quality of goods.
(ii) It reduces the cost or the product
(iii) It produces more efficacious product.
(iv) Improvement in product safety
(v) Minimization of waste
(vi) Continuous flow of product

3.11.2 Material Management

It includes movements of materials with the plant in horizontal or in vertical or in a combination of the two. It begins from procurement of raw materials and ends at the marketing of finished goods.It can be represented as follows:

Raw materials → receiving → inspection → production → packing → storage → marketing.

Material management department plays a vital role in the success of an enterprise. Around 70% of the capital invested in purchase of materials. An effective material movement has the various advantage.

3.11.3 Components of material sciences.(Pharmaceuticals)

Raw materials which include active as well as inactive materials must be packed and labeled as per the drug and cosmetic act and regulation.

The following particulars shall be either permitted or written in the indelible ink and shall appear conspicuously on the label of container of a drug or any other covering in which the container is packed.

(a) Name of drug: The proper name of drug shall be printed in a conspicuous manner than the trade name if any, which shall appear just alter or under proper name. Following preparations shall be labeled only with proper name.
   (i) Preparations containing any new drug as a single active ingredient.
   (ii) Preparations containing any drug specified in schedule 'X'as the single active ingredient.

(b) Statement of net content: In terms of weight, volume, number of units of activity etc. as the case may be.

(c) The content of active ingredients: This shall be expressed in terms of content over single dose, content per milliliter, content per tablet

(d) The name and address of the manufacturer: The name and address of the premises of the manufacturer where the drug has been manufactured.

(e) Distinctive Batch number: By reference of which details of manufacture of particular batch from which substance is taken can be made available for inspection.

(f) Manufacturing licence number: Every drug manufactured in India shall bear on its label the number of licence under which drug is manufactured.

(g) Date of manufacture: Every drug manufacture for sale bear on its label date of manufacture.

(h) Date of expiry of potency: Drugs specified in schedule P including combinations with other drugs shall bear an label "expiry date". Expiry date shall not exceed the period specified in schedule P under the conditions of storage specified therein. Per cent of alcohol should be mentioned. If physician sample then mentioned as: Physician Sample not for sale" In addition mentioned the name of schedule under which it fall.

3.11.4 Labeling of medicines mean for export

The particulars printed on the label of drugs for export shall be adapted to meet the specific requirements of law of country to which the drug is to be exported. Such drugs are exempted from the provisions of labeling of medicines. The following particulars shall appear on the label of container of medicine meant for export-

(i) Name of drugs
(ii) The name, address of manufacturer, and the manufacturing licence number.
(iii) Batch or lot number.
(iv) Date if expiry if any.

If such particular are not required by importer, the labels on package or container bear a code No approval by licensing authority.

3.12 Product Development

Product development is a specialized activity which may result in creation of new products or modifications in the production process to produce the same product. It fulfils all the added new desires as well as to adjust with the changes in the consumer's demand and also with the objective to achieve greater production, more efficacies and more profit. Details are given in the scope chapter in the beginning.

Case study 1

Case study Product modification to suit customer requirements

Dabur decided to take several initiates to cash in on the increasing purchasing power of the southern states. The company has decided to customize some of its products, reformulate and repackage them to cater to the south Indian palate, strengthen sales and distribution network in the region and even launch new products first in thee markets. Traditionally, the company neglected the southern market, focusing mainly on the northern and eastern ones because some of the power brands were not relevant to the south. But after the strong sales growth the four southern states. DIL decided to take several initiatives so that the contribution of sales from the southern region grows.

This south-focus would mean customizing products and even re-branding some of DIL's flagship products. For example, the company's largest flagship brand chyawanprash may be reformulated to suit the south Indian palate and it could be repackaged to account for language differences. In the south, Chyawanprash could even be sold as a powder. The company is conducting research to decide on the final formulation and packaging of Chyawanprash meant for the southern markets.

Other well-known brands where the re-branding option is being considered are Hajmola, Pudin Hara group of products and DaburLal Tel. The company is looking to alter brand names and packaging to cater to local needs. For example, Hajmola and DaburLal Tel are very Hindi sounding names. These brands may be re-packaged with labels in local languages.

The Vertica brand has a strong equity in the southern markets, especially in the case of coconut hair oil, and the company will use this brand extensively to focus on the region. The advertising and media spend in the south would be hoked.

Case study 2

Global Market Scenario of Biosimilars-

The global bio-similar market is driven by type of products, manufacturing, disease and origin. The products of bio-similar include non-glycosylated proteins, recombinant glycosylated proteins and recombinant peptides. In 2010. The biologics have reached

100 billion dollar with top 12 biologics generating 30 billion dollar. In 2015, biologics responsible for 30 billion dollar by annual sales claimed patent. In 2015, 20biosimilars were approved in Europe where as filgrastim bio-similar was approved by USFDA. More than 200 biologics are already in global market. 25% of the pipeline drugs are biological. It is expected that by the year 2020, worth US 19.4 billion dollar growing at a rate of 83% from 2015 to2020. It is also estimated that by 2020 out of 10 drugs 6-7 would be of biological origin.

India is one of the leading contributors of bio-similar in global market. Bio-similar production and research in India include vaccines, monoclonal antibodies, recombinant proteins, diagnostics, insulin, hormones and interferon. Recently about 100 biopharmaceutical companies are proactively involved in research, development, manufacture processing and market bio-similar products in India. There are about 14 similar biologics available in 59 different brands. Now the Indian bio-similar market is also focusing towards chronic diseases like cardic, diabetic and oncology due to complex biotech drugs. However, India cutting edge of worldwide pharmaceuticals production money owned for about 8% of all and India's contract production market is emerging3 times the charge of worldwide agreement market place.

Case Study3

New product launches

(i) **Hetero launches generic breast cancer treatment drug in India:** Drug firm Hetero has launched generic Lapatinib tablets, used in the treatment of advanced or metastatic breast cancer in the country. The tablets, under the brand name 'Hertab', have been launched in the strength of 250mg. The product is marketed and distributed by Hetero Healthcare Ltd and has been made available in two stock keeping units. The tablets are used in combination with Capecitabine or Letrozole, which together, inhibit the growth of cancer cells in patients.

(ii) **Zydus:** Cadila has received final approval from the US health regulator to market Betamethasone Dipropionate cream that is used to treat a variety of skin conditions. The group also received a final nod for Amlodipine and Atrovastin tablets USP that is administered for heart and cholesterol-related cases.BetamethasoneDipronate Cream USP 0.5% will be manufactured at the group's Topical manufacturing facility at Ahemedabad. This medication is a strong corticosteroid and used to treat a variety of skin conditions like eczema, dermatitis, allergies, and rash.

(iii) **Lupin Pharmaceuticals** has received approval for its levothyroxine sodium tablets USP, in various strengths from United States Food and Drug Administration to market a generic version of AbbVie, Ianc'sSynthroid tablets which are available in the same strength. It is indicated for Hypothyroidism as replacewment therapy in primary (thyroidal), secondary (pituitary) and tertiary (hypothalamic)congenital or acquired hypothyroidism and pituitary thyrotropin suppression as an adjunct to surgery and radioiodine therapy in the management of thyrotropin -dependent well-differentiated thyroid cancer. Levothyroxine sodium tablets had annual sales of approximately 2519.6million dollar in the US market.

UNIT 3

CHAPTER 4

SALES PROMOTION

PROMOTIONDECISION

Rural consumers are differential to elders, people in authority, and highly educated people, word of mouth promotion can play a huge role in rural markets. It is to be observed that the products are used by influential people of village .If a particular brand of fertilizers being used by the most educated and progressive farmer, all farmers will start using the same brand of fertilizer, so it is important for the company to ensure that the educated farmers of the village use its brand.

Rural consumers are very fond of quoting statements of politicians,film stars and criketers.Telivision is a good medium for celebrity endorsements but even print media is useful.Consumers are interested in local news paper for gently more information.

Now profit organizations use print media for their product promotion. Other means are direct mail or e-mailing. Sometimes they adapt the process followed by profit organizations to reach out to the eliments.

For international marketing, it is imperative that sales persons have a through knowledge of culture, customs, business practices of the foreign market in which they have to operate. The rule of international selling is to adopt the method the buyer is comfortable with or without any bias.

4.1 Domestic business marketing; comphasize on personal selling

Personal selling dominates the business marketer's promotion mix. Sales person primarily seeks to sales business customer'sproblem. Forgood promotion techniques, marketersmust have good behaviorand emphasis in advance for timely delivering of goods.

The objective of organization promotion is to prepare the customer for the sales call by presenting information about selling organization, its product lines, its customer mix and its area of specialization.

Business sales promotion makes more use of catalogues, directmail, trade shows and exhibitions. Consumer marketers use sales promotion tools like couponing,sampling and perfect purchasing sample.

Meaning

Salespromotion is a key ingredient in marketing MIX. It is an effective sales tool. It consists of a collection of incentives tools, designed to stimulate greater purchases of particular product or services by consumers or the trade. It includes tools for

(a) Consumer promotion

(b) Trade promotion

(c) Sales force promotion.

4.1.1 Consumer promotion

includes (i) samples (ii) (iii) cash refund offers (iv) prizes (v) premium process and warranties (vi) demonstration.

Samples: offer of a free amount of a product delivered door to door, sent in the mail, picked up in a store or attached to another product in a advertising offer.

Coupons: certificates entitling the bearer to a stated saving on the purchase of a specific product, mailed enclosed in other products or attached to them or inserted in magazine or newspaper ads.

Cash refund offers: provide a price reduction after purchase rather than at the retail shop. Consumer sends a specific proof of purchase to the manufacture that refunds part of the purchase price by mail.

Prizes: are offers of the chance to win cash, trips or merchandise as a result of purchasing something. A contest calls for consumers to submit or entry to be examined by a panel of judges who will select the best entries.

Warranties: Explicit or implicit promises by sellers that the product will perform as specific or that the seller will fix it or refund the customer's money during a specific period of time.

4.1.2 Trade promotion

Manufacturer use a number of trade promotion tools to consumer. To persuade the retailer or wholesalers to buy the brand. Itincludes i) advertising ii) display allowances iv) free goods.

Advertising: it offers a reason to buy to a consumer. It can be used to build up a long term image for a product or trigger quick sales. Advertising can efficiently reach geographically dispersed buyers.

Allowance: An amount offered in return for the retailer's agreeing to feature the manufacturer 'products in some way. An advertising allowance compensates retails for advertising the manufacturer's product. A display allowance compensates them for carrying a special product display.

Free goods: offer of extra cases of merchandise to intermediaries who buy a certain quantity or who feature a certain flavor or size.

4.1.3 Sales force promotion

These to gather business leads, impress and reward customers, and motivate the sales force to gather tools are used effort. Companies typically develop budgets for each business promotion tool that remain fairly constant from year to year. It includes i) trade shows ii) conventions iii) contests

Trade shows: Business marketers may spend as much as 35% of their annual promotion budget on trade shows. Several benefits including generating new sales leads, maintaining customer contact introducing new products.

Sales contests: A sale contest aims at inducing the sales force or dealers to increase their sales results over a stated period with prizes going to those who succeed.

Conventions: Where important buyers are called to attain to know the benefits of the products through presentation or any special discussion. Participating members expect to know several benefits.

4.2 Objectives

Sales promotion tools vary in their specific objectivesFree samples stimulates consumer trial where as free management advisory services aims at converting a long-term relation-ship with a retailer. Sellers use incentives type promotions to attract new buyers to reward loyal customers and to increase the repurchase rates of occasional users. Product branding is another way to promote the product to the customers. Brand name attracts the customers who are looking for low priced value or premiums. Sales promotion may be able to alter market shows permanently. In addition brand can switch the consumers from one product to another product having in mind that it is superior to qualities.

4.3 Determinant of promotional mix

Sales promotion objectives are derived from broader promotion objectives, which are derived from more basic marketing objectives developed for the product. Objective includes encouraging purchase of larger-sizes units, building trial among nonusers and attracting switchers away from competitors 'brands.

4.3.1 Selection of consumer promotion tools

The planner should take into account the type of market, sales promotion objectives, competitive conditions and each tool's cost-effectiveness. The main consumer promotion tools are free sample, cash discount, cash refund, coupons, premium(gifts), prizes,wrarranties and cross promotion. There is a distinguish between manufacturer promotions and retailer promotions. The former use of rebates, gifts and high value trade in credit. The latter include price cuts, feature advertising, retailer coupons and retailer contests or premiums.

4.3.2 Selection of trade promotion tools

Manufacturers use a number of trade promotion tools like allowances, free goods and price off. Surprisingly a higher proportion of the promotion pie is devoted to trade promotion tools than to consumer promotion. Manufacturers awarded money to the trade i) to persuade the retailer or wholesaler to carry the brand ii) to persuade the retailer or wholesaler to carry more units than the normal amounts iii) to induce retailer to promote the brand by featuring, display and price reduction and iv) to stimulate retailers and their sales clerks to push the product.

4.4 Promotion technique for OTC (over the counter) products.

OTC products are those that are available to consumers without a prescription. There are more than 80 therapeutic categories of OTC drugs, ranging from anti-acne drugs to weight control drugs. As with the prescription drugs, Centre of drug evaluation and research over sees OTC drugs to ensure that they are properly labeled and that their benefits outweigh their risks.OTC drugs generally have these characteristics:

(i) Their benefits outweigh their risks.

(ii) The potential for misuse and abuse is low.

(iii) Consumers can use them for self-diagnosed conditions.

(iv) They can be adequately labeled.

(v) Health practitioners are not needed for the safe and effective use of these drugs.

These products are marketed by two regulations likely

(a) NDA (new drug application) described in 21 CFR (code of federal regulation) part 314.

(b) OTC drug monograph regulation described in 21CFRPart 330.

OTC drugs marketed under either mechanism must meet the established standards for safety and effectiveness. Products must be manufacturedaccording to current good manufacturing practices (cGMP) as defines in 21 CFR Part 210 and must comply with the labeling content and format requirements in 21CFR Part 201 subpart C.

An OTC drug label must contain the following information:

(i) Name of the active ingredients

(ii) Information on uses.

(iii) Warning
(iv) Inactive ingredients used.
(v) Purposes.
(vi) Directions for use
(vii) Storage conditions

All these products are sold having the following information like:

(i) Keep out the reach of the children.
(ii) In case of overdose, get medical help a poison control center.
(iii) If any changes related to active ingredients, directions for use, warning or precautions are made to label than the change must be flagged to identify such changes.
(iv) other requirements like it must be tamper resistant packaging.

4.5 Advertisement

Advertising is structuredinformation, used to intimate the user about the product. Information of its uses, sources of availability and prices. It is not merely propaganda but is a paid form of communication.

4.5.1 Objectives

(i) to aware the name of the product.
(ii) to generate a demand by explaining its utility.
(iii) to increase its sale by attracting new customers.
(iv) to maintain the existing demand by fighting competition.
(v) to enhance goodwill of the firm.
(vi) to build and retaining brand loyalty.

4.5.2 Advantages of advertising

i) It helps in introducing of new products in the market.
(ii) It helps in creating a demand and hence a regular production.
(iii) It helps a firm to face competition in the market for its survival.
(iv) It promotes the sale of goods and services by persuading the people to buy them.
(v) It enables a firm to improve its reputation by highlighting its achievements to the customers.
(vi) It generates employment for artists and other persons in the line.
(vii) It provides revenue to newspaper,magazines,doordarshan and radio.
(viii) It enables manufacturers to expand the market
(ix) It helps in maintaining uniformity and stability of prices.

4.5.3 Dis-advantages

(i) It increasing the cost of the product.
(ii) It involves a huge wasteful expenditure because many time people ignore it.
(iii) It simply shifts demand from one company to another.
(iv) Sometimes it induces the customers to buy it but they really do not need it.

4.5.4 Parts of advertisement

(a) Heading/Title: Generally it the name of the product. It may be a word, a phrase or even a question about the product or the service being advertised. It should not be very long.

(b) Theme: Theme gives the basic ides about the product and highlights its distinctive advantage. It conveys an image of the product being advertising. For example D-cold tablet contains the theme of effective against cough and symptoms of cold. Vitazyme means it contains vitamin and enzyme. Moov ointment contains the theme of effective against backache.

(c) Picture: Generally a photo of a product is being advertised during advertising. It combines with a photo of the model possessing or using it. It enables the customers to recognize or identify the product.

(d) Arguments: Now a day arguments in favour of advertised product are given in the advertisement. The purpose of giving the argument is to convince the customers about the product's utility.

(e) Closing part: The closing part of the advertisement is very often repeats in brief the contents of advertisement. In some cases the name and address of the drug store where the product is available are given in this part.

4.5.5 Essential features

(i) It should be attractive by using pictures, cartons so as to make people read it.
(ii) It should create a permanent impression on the minds of people who use it
(iii) It should give useful suggestions to the public.
(iv) It should educate the people about its use and benefits.
(v) Itshould create the need for the product in the mind of people.
(vi) It should induce people to buy the product.
(vii) Languages used should be easily understandable to the customers.

4.5.6 Limitations of advertisement of a pharmaceutical product

The purpose of advertising the pharmaceutical products is the same as that for any other product but there are many restriction on it. World Health Organization (WHO) has given some restriction as below:

"The advertising the pharmaceutical products should be truthful. There should not be any wrong statement regarding its contents and their content percentage. It should provide full details regarding the action and uses, proprietary name as well as the generic name, dosage form, mode of administration, side effects. Treatment of toxic effects, precautions and contraindications. The above statement should be truthful, scientifically correct and proved".

A customer (patient) cannot buy directly from the medicine shop without the prescription of a medical practitioner, or a physician. The majority of the pharmaceutical products are ethical and their direct advertisements prohibited according to the Drugs and Magic Remedies Act. However general or OTC products such as pain balm, inhalers Iodoex, antiseptic creams which do not require a prescription for the purchase can be advertise by any of the direct method of advertisement.

The following methods are used for advertisement of pharmaceutical product:

1. Direct mailing.
2. Newspaper. Professional magazine, journals.
3. Television, Radio.and other visual media
4. Personal contact
5. Out-door advertisement
6. Miscellaneous methods.

Direct mailing

New drug informationare sent to the registered medical practitioners, chemists and druggists for their support for marketing. By mailing the manufacturers kept their contact with the doctors. They send the leaflets, letters, folders and catalogues regularly and informed them of the details of the product. Mail advertising has a personal appeal because it is addressed to particular persons. It also maintain secrecy in advertising. The main drawback of this technique is that it has a limited coverage.

Advantages

(i) Advertising through mail require minimum expenses.
(ii) It is very useful for those doctors who live in the distance from the city.
(iii) There is a direct link between manufacturer and the doctor.
(iv) Doctors get information while sitting in the home.
(v) Doctors can send their views directly to the manufacturers.

Disadvantages

(i) Doctors cannot examine the medicines before prescribing to the patients.
(ii) As there is no direct personal contact with doctor so it is difficult to make permanent customers.
(iii) There are chances of cheating by a dishonest trader.
(iv) Doctors who want to make enquiries, may face problem.

Television, radio and other audio visual media

Television is the latest and fast growing medium of advertising. It is a very effective medium because it appeals to both the eye and the ear. The product can be demonstrated and explain very easily. Radio advertisement is becoming more popular these days and advertisements are generally transmitted through commercial services of All India Radio. This is very effective as they reach out to all sections of society. People can listen to them even when they are Busy with other activities. The large pharmaceutical companies generally sponsor entertaining programs on TC and radio to popularise themselves and their products.

Outdoor advertisement

This type of advertisement is becoming very popular now-a-days. It means the exhibition of an advertisement at street corners, railway station, bus stands on moving vehicle etc. Outdoor advertisement is carried in a number of ways to attract the attention of the passers-by.

Promotional mix

1. Free sample
2. Trading Stamps
3. Coupons
4. Premium/bonus offer
5. Prize contests
6. Fairs and exhibitions
7. Price reduction
8. Indoor display
9. Outdoor display.

Free sample: Many pharmaceutical companies send their medical representatives to the physicians for detailing and distribution of free samples of their products. The technique is very popular and useful to introducing the new products. However it is a very expensive method and is used only by big firms.

4.6 Recruitment, Training, Evaluation and Compensation

Recruitment: Is the process of searching prospective candidates to apply for jobs in the organization. It is the process to stimulate the prospective candidate to apply for the job. Its other purpose is to create a pool of candidates from which the most suitable persons may be selected for the job. A well-organized selection procedure has to be adopted to select suitable candidates for various jobs. The following selection procedure is generally adopted.

(a) **Scrutiny of application:** The applications received up to date are carefully for various scrutinized. The incomplete applications and applications of candidates who do not fulfill the required eligibility conditions are rejected.

(b) **Preliminary interview:** The candidate considered suitable on the basis of their application are called for preliminary interview. This is generally a brief interview and its purpose is to eliminate that candidate who is either unqualified or unsuitable for the job.

(c) **Selection test:** It may be written or an oral test depending of the number of candidates appearing for the interview. The technical and administrative capability can be judged from these tests. The psychological tests are very popular these days to judge human behavior in actual work situations. The following tests are commonly used in the selection process.

(i) **Intelligent tests:** These tests are used to estimate the IQ or mental alertness of the candidate.

(ii) **Aptitude tests:** These tests help to measure a candidate's capacity to learn particular skills and his potential abilities.

Trade tests: these tests are designed to measure the applicant's level of knowledge and skill already achieved in a particular trade or occupation. These tests are also known as performance tests or proficiency tests.

(iii) **Personality tests-** These tests are employed to find out the emotional balance, maturity, temperament of the candidate.

(d) **Selection interview:** A face-to-face dialogue between the employer or his representatives and the interest candidate is the most popular tool of selection. the main purpose of a selection interview is to find out the suitable candidate, to cross check the information revealed in the application and tests., to give to the candidate an accurate picture of his job and enterpriser.

(e) **Physical Examination:** It is to ensure that he is physically fit for the job.

(f) **Reference check:** Usually the candidate is required to write in their names and addresses in their application. It helps the company to know more about the candidates.

(g) **Final selection and placement:** During final selection no such subject matter are asked. Mostly the about the facilities the candidate wants and the company would provide are discussed. It also highlight about his future prospects. In the company. Place of work also to be discussed.

Case Study 1

It is important to consider the impact of a sales promotion campaign on the total cost of a product.

When a company evaluates the cost of a sales promotion campaign, it focuses its attention mostly on marketing costs. A typical sales campaign raises the volume of products that have to be manufactured during the time the sale is on, and the volume gets reduced after the sales period is over as some consumers may have also bought for future consumption periods due to the lower prices. Since the cost of productions is lowest when production is at optimum level rather than too above or below it, a sales promotion campaign will always result in higher per unit cost. In addition the company may also incur some inventory storage cost. Since the effective selling price is already lower, this extra per unit cost will put profit margins under great pressure.

Case Study 2

Advertisement is the one of the powerful tools to strengthen the sale promotion.

Use advertising to strengthen brand image and to counter sales promotions by competitors.There is a proliferation of brands, and most brands are indulging in sales promotion. Under such hostile circumstances it is very important to prevent one's customers from switching over to those brands that a rival brand when it is on sale. Companies that want to sell at normal prices for most of the year and do not want their customers to get poached should advertise extensively. Though advertising does not give the spurt in sales that sales promotion is likely to give, it is very effective in stopping customers from switching to.

Case Study 3

Importance of product branding.

Sales promotions give the myth of higher revenue. In fact, there may be revenue losses from loyal customers, while deal prone consumers may not compensate enough for this loss.

A reasonably good brand will have a large numbers of customers who would have bought the brand at the higher price had the sales promotion campaign not taken place. Therefore from a large numbers of customers the revenue realization is lower than normal. In addition some of these consumers would buy for future periods at these lower prices during the sales, resulting in further depression in revenues as compared to the revenues that could have been received from these customers at normal prices in the next consumption period. And for the most goods consumption does not increase just because the price is lower. Therefore the company's sales to its loyal customer does not increase but the revenue realization is reduced. This revenue deficit can be compensated for by the surplus that can be expected to come from customers who will switch from other brands. It is very dangerous to rely on data of brand switchers of the last sales promotion campaign and the behavior of these brand switchers is very existential in nature. How many of the brand switchers will buy a particular brand again will depend on other sales promotion campaigns available in the market. However because of the multitude of sales promotion campaign operating at one time, brand switchers may not be able to bring that extra revenue.

Case Study 4

Advertising power is in the dialogue delivered.

Speech cans ordinary advertisement dramatic, sublime and memorable. Advertising power is often in the dialogue delivered. A few adroitly crafted words can paint a compelling picture of the brand's benefit.

Sometimes it is the verbal virtuosity that transforms a mundane advertisement into a masterpiece. A fast-talking,absolutely sure of himself, and stickler for the right words, presenter can mesmerize viewers and leave them gasping. The message hits the viewer hard.

At other times, it is the confessional and conspiratorial nature of the dialogue that makes the viewer curious and interested in knowing the full details. He concentrates hard lest he misses the juicy and the spicy sound bytes.

Scripted conversations can be so skillfully performed that the customers may believe that they are watching in real life. Some couples and friends have looked so authentic on screen that viewers assume them to be couples or friends in real life too. Messages from such 'real' people are more believable. Sometimes incongruous mixing of words and action creates a startling disconnect that viewers immediately take a note of. This moment of extreme attentiveness is used to deliver a message to the viewers.

Oratory has always been a powerful medium for communication, but with the television audience right up there in the space where in the action is taking place, high pitch and elaborate body movements is just one of the possible modes of delivering a dialogue. The dialogue delivery can take many forms and shades but dialogue is still as important for moving people today as it was during Roman Empire.

UNIT 4

CHAPTER 5

PHARMACEUTICAL MARKETING CHANNELS

CHANNEL

The manufacturer has to select the inter-mediatory who will carry his products. The chosen intermediaries have to be trained in specific areas like the working of product being carried,art of selling,merchanding area in other areas depending on the requirement of the business.A company has to consider many factors related to the market and customers, its own situation the product and the competitive environment. All of these factors have a strong bearing on the type of distribution channel selected.

5.1 Types of distribution channels

Industrial channels tend to be shorter than consumer channels because of small number of ultimate customers greater complexity of the product which require close manufacturer –customer understanding.

Consumer channels are normally longer because a large number of geographically dispersed customers have to be reached. The consumers buy in small quantities.

1. **ConsumerChannels:** Manufacture may reach out to consumers either directly in without using distribution channel or by using one or more distribution channels member.

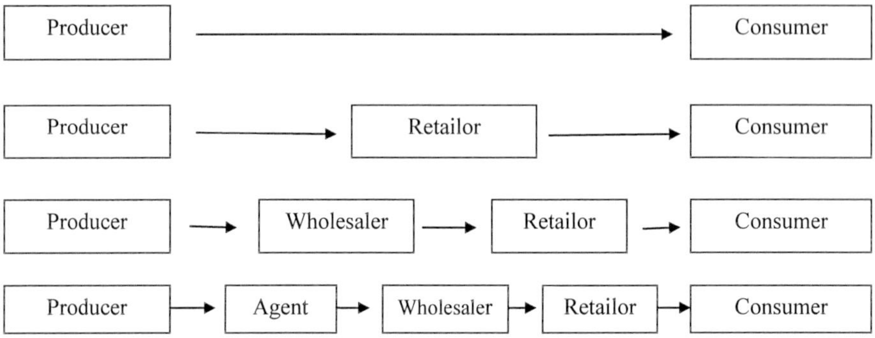

The type of channel used depends on customer requirements such as level of perceived risk about the product, the customer's knowledge about the product, his delivery and service requirements. Usually R&D (research &development) products have longer distribution channels while consumer durable have shorter distribution channel.

Industrial channel: Industrial channels are usually shorter than consumer channels. Direct selling is prevalent due to closer relationship between the manufacturer and the customer as well as due to the nature of the product sold.

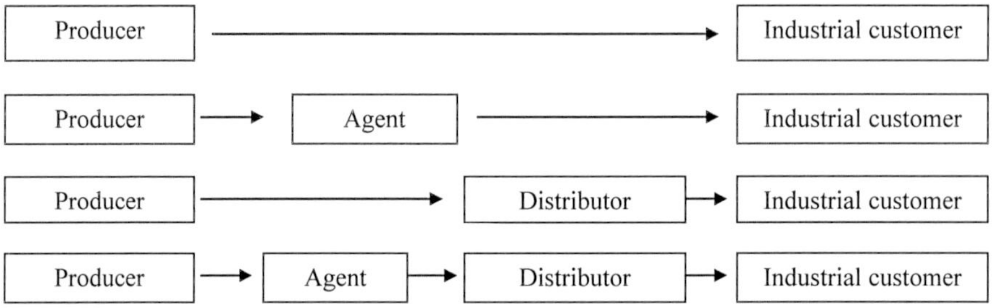

Manufacturer to industrial customers in a common channel for expensive industrial produces like heavy equipment and machine.

Service channel: Distribution channels for services are usually short are either direct or by using an agent. Since stocks are not lead, the role of whole sales, retailers or industrial distributors does not apply.

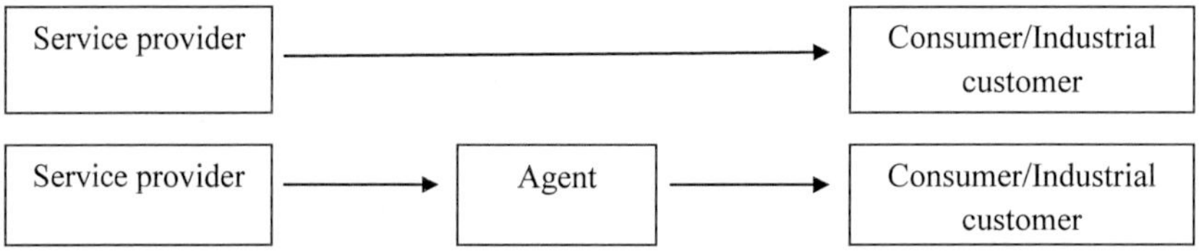

Pharmaceutical Distribution Channel

The main objective of pharmaceutical distribution channel is to provide adequate quantities of products in convenience locations and at right time when patient want to buy them. Channel includes all those organizations that facilitate the distribution of products from producers to customers. Producers need to consider not only the needs of the patients who are the ultimate consumer but also requirements of intermediaries like stockiest, distributors and retailers.

5.1.1 Design of distribution channel:

Type I

Manufacturer
↓
Retailer

Type II

Manufacturer
↓
Distributor
↓
Retailer

Type III

Manufacturer
↓
Stockiest
↓
Distributor
↓
Retailer

5.2 Channel Members

Pharmaceutical products like various dosage forms and diagnostics kits are handled by competent technical persons (pharmacists). Pharmacists are designated as various names like retail pharmacists or druggists, distributor pharmacists, wholesale pharmacists. Medical field executives (medical representatives) play an important role for selling of pharmaceutical products. Having the knowledge of pharmacology, preservation and distribution systems they convince the physicians for prescribing their medicines to the patients. Channel members take the main role to provide those medicines easily nearer to their residences.

First important channel member is the **manufacturer** who realize the formulation of the items from the market survey. How much quantity to be formulate at what time and also at what price that they know from those channel members.

Second important indirect channel member is the **doctor** who feel to need of the patient of that medicines.

Other subsequent members are **distributors, retailers** who make the continuous flow of medicines to the patients.

5.2.1 Retailers duty

A retailer is a middle man between a wholesaler and actual consumer. Here the druggists acts as retailer and patient is the consumer. They always keep contact with wholesalers, manufacturer and the consumers. They have the following functions –

(i) Pharmacists keep a stock of various kinds of medicines according to the needs of the patients.

(ii) They are suppose to know the application of different kinds of medicines likely to be demanded by his patients recommendation by medical practitioners.

(iii) He also know the sources where the same could be obtained.

(iv) Retailer mainly make their own arrangement for transportation of products from the wholesaler go downs.

(v) Normally during storing gradation of goods are done by producer name or sometimes by wholesalers. However a retailer dose grading of those goods which have been left ungraded by the manufacturer and wholesalers.

(vi) Retailer has to maintain a reasonable stock of goods. They bear the risk of loss of goods by fire, theft or deterioration as long as they are not sold.

(vii) Sometimes they provide financial help to consumers by selling them the goods on credit.

(vii) They keep close contact with their doctors who know the likes and dislikes of the prescribe medicines. In this regard marketing professionals (medical representatives) play an important role to convince the doctor. They pass on such information to the wholesalers for onward transmission to the manufacturers concerned.(mainly patient's complaints via doctor).

(viii) A retailer helps to promote the sale of goods manufactured by a particular manufacturer who has launched the sale promotion campaign by display the goods in show windows and on counter for the information of the customers.

5.2.2 Wholesaler duty

(i) Wholesaler communicates the customer's views about their products problems (merits and demerits) to the manufacturer.

(ii) Product advertising is mainly done both by the manufacturer and distributors.

(iii) Wholesalers are interested in the sale of popular products and they are not interested with the new product.

(iv) Wholesalers help the manufacturer to estimate the demand of their products in future, because they have a well knit network of retailers.

(v) Financial problems arise both from producers as well as retailers that can be eliminated by wholesalers. Retailers able to purchase goods on credit.

(vi) Free shop delivery is possible by wholesalers.

5.2.3 Medical Representative duty

They act as commission agents of the drug manufacturers. They sell goods on behalf of the seller. They negotiate with the doctors for prescribing their medicines and take the possession of the supplying the same in time through retailer. Mainly they do the following jobs.

(i) As they are qualified, gets intensive coaching and training on both product knowledge and selling processes. The success of a firm mainly depends on their performances.

(ii) They must have an attractive personality with goods health and sound physiques.

(iii) A pleasing and charming personality creates a good impression on doctors.

(iv) He must have the imagination to look at things from the view point of customer.

(v) He should possess a sound memory, presence of mind and imaginative power. He has a liking for people and ability to convince the doctors.

(vi) He has the patience to listen the various retailers and doctors to remove their objections.

(vii) He always be polite and courteous while dealing with his customers. Courtesy costs nothing but wins favor and permanent customers.

(viii) He must has specialized knowledge of selling techniques.

5.3 Channel selection strategy

A company has to consider many factors related to the market and customers, its own situation, the product and the competitive custom investment.All these factors strong bearing on the type of distribution channel selected.

5.3.1 Marketing factors

While selecting the distribution channels, companies must take into consideration factors such as the availability of channel members,buying patterns and location of the consumers, powder distribution in the distribution channels and the company's own ability to serve customers.

5.3.2 Manufacturer factors

Company's financial resources affect channel selection .It may be cost effective to select direct marketing if a company offers a wide win of products for the same customer. The company must also decide the degree of control that it wants to have over the channel members.

5.3.3 Productfactors

The nature of the product affects the level of efficiency and responsiveness of the channel. Perishable, fashion and technology produces require responsive supply chain where as stable products like FMCG (First Moving Consumable Goods) and durable products require efficient supply chain.

5.3.4 Competitivefactors

A sales force may be recreated to sell directly its competition control traditional channels of distribution or a manufacturer controlled or owned distribution network may be set up. Producers should not accept that channels of distribution used by competitors are the only way to read target customers. Alternative distribution channels may be used as a means of attaining competitive average.

5.3.5 Selling of the product

It largely depends on the motivation of intermediaries who eagerly push the manufacturer'sproduct. The manufacturer may offer him financial and non-financial indicating. It is important that the intermediaries are evaluated periodically in terms of the functions that they are required to perform.

Finally manufacturer has to resolve conflicts arising among members at the same level or among member at different levels of the distribution channel.

5.3.5.1 Identifying sources

Sources for identifying candidates include trade associations, exhibitions, trade publications, reseller enquiries and customers of distributions. Sometimes channel members may be proactive in contacting a manufacturer to express an interest in analyzing their products.

5.3.5.2 Depending selection criteria

Common selection criteria include market, product and customer knowledge market coverage, quality and size of sales force, reputation among customers and financial standing.

5.3.5.3 Motivating

For motivation one has to understand the needs and problems of distributors. Some distributors may value financial incentives, others may prefer exclusive territorial rights. Possible motivators are financial incentives, territorial exclusivity, providing resource support(additional, promotional support)strong work relationship.

5.3.5.4 Training

Training provides necessary technical knowledge about manufacturer and its products and helps to built a spirit of partnership and commitments. Retailer or distributors both may welcome the training efforts by manufacturer.

5.4 Conflict in channels

In view the important services rendered by wholesalers/stockiest it is not desirable to eliminate them as they act as an important link man between manufacturer and consumer.

Conflict in favors of channels

The price of the product increases due to presence of wholesalers as they are paying by the manufacturer.

Producer can sell their products to consumers through advertisement without the help of distributor.

Wholesalers are only interested in selling of popular products but not the newer product.

The retailer can easily buy required quantity of goods from producer directly.

Sometimes wholesaler creates the scarcity in the market by hoarding the product. Due to shortage of supply the prices get increased in the market. Thus wholesalers exploit the consumers by charging very high prices.

Cooperative societies are increasing day by day. These societies earn less rate of profit and sell better qualities goods at reasonable prices by purchasing directly from producers.

Conflict against channels

Producer does not get the amount goods required for future uses. This information is supplied by wholesalers, because they have a well knit network of retailers.

Wholesalers provide various services to the retailers regarding marketing of goods which may not be possible for the retailers to perform it.

If wholesalers are eliminated, the retailers will not be able to purchase goods on credit. Similarly producer will not be able to get advances from wholesalers. Hence both producers as well as retailers will have to face financial difficulties.

Wholesalers provide free shop delivery facility to the retailers which may not be possible in absence of wholesalers.

Lastly in absence of wholesalers the retailers would purchase goods in small quantities from producers. This will lead to increase in expenses on additional packing and transport etc.

5.5 Physical distribution management

Physical distribution management involves distribution programming which can be defined as building a planned, professionally managed; vertical marketing system. It meets the needs of both manufacturer and distributor. The manufacturer job in this regard is to identify distributor's needs and builds up merchandising programs to help each distributor operate as efficiently as possible. They help the distributors to maintain inventory level, space and sale-training requirements and advertising and promotion plans. The aim is to convert the distributors from thinking that they make their money primarily on the buying side to seeing that they make their money on selling side. A manufacturer selling physical product and services might require three channels namely a sales channel, a delivery channel and a service channel. A sale channel includes television infomercials, the telephone and the internet. Delivery channels include transporter and warehousing. A service channel includes experts or repair personnel or medical representatives who describe the benefits installation of the item to the customers.

All channels functions have three things in common like specialized personnel, resources to move materials and space to accommodate goods.

Physical distribution of pharmaceutical goods like medicines, cosmetics, toiletries and diagnostics kits are done by two types of retailers-

(A) Itinerant retailers (B) Fixed shop retailers.

5.5.1 Itinerant retailers

It include hawkers paddlers, street traders, market traders. Hawkers normally sell the small and cheap item such antifungal ointments, painkilling ointment or lotion, bum and over the counter product. Street traders generally arrange their goods at busy street corners or pavements of busy roads, temples, railway station cinema halls etc. They generally deal only in one particular line of products examples are hazmola tablets or pain killing ointments.Market traders keep on moving from place to place to sell their goods at weekly, fortnightly or monthly bazaar or at annual fair.

5.5.2 Fixed shop retailers

The fixed shop retailers set up permanent establishment to sell their goods. They do not go from place to place in search of their customers. In fact it is the customers who visit the shop to get their requirements. The fixed shop retailers may be divided into two sub-groups namely

(a) Small scale retail shop
(b) Large scale retail shop.

Small scale retail shops include general store, single line store, and specialty store.

General stores are present in the residential area. There remain all kinds of medicines needed by the local doctors for their general kinds of patients. They are the boon to the local people, particularly to those who are living in far flung colonies. In their absence, the patients would have to run to the central market for such minor purchases such as tooth paste, toilet soaped. They are owned and managed by a single individual.

5.5.3 Strategic importance

One of the main roles of distribution is to increase the sale volume and material safety during transportation and storing the items. Management needs to search for distribution economics in inventory control, warehouse location and transportation modes. It should track such measures as:

(i) Logistic costs s a percentage of sales.
(ii) Percentage of orders filled correctly.
(iii) Percentage of on-time delivery.
(iv) Number of billing errors.

Management should strive to reduce inventory while at the same time speeding up the order to delivery cycle. Each company should periodically reassess its strategic approaches to the market place with marketing effectiveness review.

5.5.4 Tasks in physical distribution management

Physical distribution management discovers weaknesses in their distribution system through a study known as marketing audit. A market audit is a comprehensive, systematic, independent and periodic examination of a company's marketing environment, objectives strategies and activities with a view to determine problem areas and opportunities recommending a plan of action to improve the company's market performances. There are four main characteristics of marketing audit like:

(i) Comprehensive: The marketing audit covers all the major marketing activities of business. It would be called a functional audit if it covers only the sale forces, pricing or distributors.

(ii) Systematic: The marketing audit is an orderly examination of the organization's macro and micro market environment. Marketing objective and strategies, marketing systems and specific activities.

(iii) Independent: A markets audit can be conducted in six ways- self audit. Audit from across, a audit from above, company auditing office, company task force audit and out sider audit.

(v) Periodic: Typically marketing audit are initiated only after sale have turned down and sale force moral has fallen and other problems have occurred.

5.5.5 Evaluation

By evaluation one could understand which channel members to retain and which to drop. Shortfalls in distributors and skills, competitor are identified through evaluation. Evaluation may be managing conflict; limited where power lies with various members of the distribution channel. Set goals that they want to achieve. Channel conflicts occur where one member of the distribution channel perceives that some other member is presently the fifth members from achieving.

5.6 On line marketing

Rules about pharmacies' and authorized retailers' online sale of medicines

According to the Danish rules on online sale of medicines, medicines may only be marketed or dispensed in Denmark when a marketing authorisation has been granted. If a medicinal product is to be marketed to users in other European countries, a marketing authorisation applicable in the country of destination is required.A medicinal product is not necessarily placed in the same dispensing group in the various European countries.

Some countries may, unlike other countries, have placed a medicinal product in a dispensing group, which implies that only specialists in a specific area are authorised to prescribe the medicine.

Overall, pharmacies selling medicines online must comply with all the rules applicable to pharmacies' sale of medicines to consumers. Pharmacies are obliged to offer substitution of medicines and inform consumers of less expensive alternatives, also in connection with online sale.

Distributors authorised to sell medicines by retail in accordance with section 39(1) of the Danish Medicines Act and who sell such medicines online are also obliged to comply with all the rules applicable to the distribution of medicines.

Executive order no. 675 of 20 May 2015 on pharmacies' and retailers' online sale and on distribution of medicinal products lays down additional rules.

A pharmacy must provide information about medicines and offer oral and written advice on the website from which it sells medicines online. This means that consumers must be able to contact the pharmacy by telephone and in writing via the website. Consumers must be able to contact the pharmacy during the normal opening hours, as a minimum.

The website must be accessible for disabled consumers, primarily consumers with a visual impairment or other reading difficulties. The website must also inform consumers, who have problems reading or understanding the text, that they can contact the pharmacy by telephone or physically during the pharmacy's opening hours if they need more information.

In Denmark, a pharmacy's website must not make it possible for consumers to have an online consultation with a doctor or dentist to obtain a prescription and order medicines on the website.

Compensation

Medicines are supposed to prevent, relieve or cure diseases. Yet sometimes, it occurs that a medicine does harm. Money cannot change this, but compensation for personal damage may ease the situation a little.

When you buy a medicine from a Danish pharmacy or other authorised retailer in Denmark, you are automatically covered by insurance for pharmaceutical injuries. If you have bought a medicine outside Denmark, you cannot be sure to receive compensation. Even the 'money back guaranty' can easily be broken by the online retailer.

You must also be aware that there are rules restricting the possibility for private individuals to receive medicines dispatched from foreign countries, i.e.. including medicines purchased online. It is illegal to receive medicines purchased or dispatched from a country outside the European.Moreover, it is only permitted to import medicines that are purchased legally and for personal use.

It is also illegal to receive medicines containing **euphoriant substances** or **doping agents**

Good advice

There are a number of conditions to be aware of when shopping online, especially when it comes to medicines. We have gathered a handful of tips that makes it a little easier to comprehend online shopping.

Choose your online retailer carefully

Many shops sell medicines on the internet. It is important to find a serious and reliable online retailer, but it is not necessarily easy. Here are a few questions; you can ask yourself when assessing an online retailer:

- Is it apparent who is behind the website and the information, products and services offered?
- If the website contains advertisements, are they then separated from the information?
- Has the website been updated recently?

Moreover, there are some signs that should make you suspicious:

- When promises of health and recovery are too good to be true
- When there are long lists of various diseases that a single medicine can cure
- When the medicine can only be purchased at that specific retailer or only for a limited period

Insist on information about the medicine

As a customer, you are entitled to precise information on the medicine you are considering to buy. If you do not receive adequate information about the medicine, you should find a more serious retailer.

Adequate and factual information will include details about, e.g.:

- Name of the medicine
- Active substances
- Therapeutic indications (what the medicine is used for)
- When the medicine must not be used (e.g. during pregnancy or concurrently with other medicines)
- Dosage
- Any possible side effects
- The manufacturer's name and address

Only buy authorised medicines

In Denmark and other European countries, medicines must be authorised by the health authorities before it is permitted to sell them to consumers. If you have doubts, asks the retailer whether the medicine is authorised, and if yes: In which countries?

If the retailer does not know whether the medicine is authorised or refuses to answer, something is very wrong.

What about the package leaflet?

When you buy medicines in Denmark, the package and package leaflet are in Danish. The package leaflet includes important information about the medicine, e.g. effect and side effects, warnings, storage instructions, specific precautions that you should pay attention. .When you buy a medicine outside Denmark, you should ensure that you receive a package leaflet in a familiar language.

Beware of name confusion

Medicines often have different names in different countries. Therefore, you cannot be sure that the packages contain the same even though the names may sound very alike. If you are unsure about a specific medicine, then ask an acquaintance who knows about medicines, ask the pharmacy, or try to compare the active substances with a medicine you know.

Avoid counterfeit medicines

Anything can be counterfeited, including medicines. If you buy medicines online, you will often not know who the retailer is. It is also difficult to determine whether the retailer is subject to any type of regulatory control in the country where the retailer is established.This means that there is a risk that your purchase is not what you think it is. In best case, the medicine is ineffective. In worst case, it is outright damaging.

Will you receive compensation?

Medicines are supposed to prevent, relieve or cure diseases. Yet sometimes, it occurs that a medicine does harm. Money cannot change this, but compensation for personal damage may ease

Case Study 1

The channel structure is determined by the life of the product and customers 'business practices and needs.

The channels of distribution can be alarming long and complex. It is uncommon for an auto part to move through five or six wholesalers and retailers totheir customers. The structure and length of the channel depends on their way to customers. The structure and length of the channel depends on the tasks to be performed. And the tasks to be performed depend on the marketing needs and nature of the product, consumer buying practices and needs, and the company goals and competitive situation. The product itself determines many of the demands to be placed on the channel. Because supplies for some medical instrumentation require refrigeration; the channel of distribution must be capable of providing it. Products with fast obsolescence due to either product perishables or to fashion perishables place demands on speed of response. The ultimate consumers 'needs have a major impact on the channels. Some industrial equipment may be so important to the customers 'manufacturing process that it must be repaired quickly. Thus the manufacturer needs to provide local service.

Case Study 2

Logistics functions are being centralized to improve co-ordination.

In the past, most companies managed the inbound transportation of raw materials and the outbound transportation of finished products as two separate functions, and each business unit managed its own logistics activities. This arrangement was thought promote flexibility. But the needs to cater to far flung markets, increased outsourcing and new technologies have changed the equation. Companies are consolidating their logistics at their headquarters. A central group manages all shipping and distribution and establishes uniform standards across the organization. An organization needs to build a strong competency in logistics at the headquarters to be able to orchestrate and manage the ever-widening network external relationships required in global supply chains. Information technologies allow a small group of employees at the headquarters to manage a lot of data from many sources.

Companies are also entering into more long-term exclusive contracts with fewer carriers such as trucking companies and railroads. Having fewer relationships allow them to measure quality and costs better. Companies are also outsourcing parts of the function. A large third-party logistics provider can lower a company's cost even further through volume purchases of transportation and related services. This will require controls to be tightened further.

Case Study 3

The channel structure is determined by the nature of the product and customers' buying practices and needs.

The channels of distribution can be alarmingly long and complex. It is not uncommon for an auto part to move through five or six wholesalers and retailers on their way to customers. The structure and length of the channel depends on the tasks to be performed. And the tasks to be performed depend on the marketing needs and nature of the product, consumer buying practices and needs, and the company goals and competitive situation. The product itself determines many of the demands to be placed on the channel. Because supplies for some medical instrumentation require refrigeration, the channel of distribution must be capable of providing it. Products with fast obsolescence due to either product perishability or to perishability place demands on speed of response. The ultimate consumers' needs have a major impact on the channels. Some industrial equipment may be so important to the customers' manufacturing process that it must have repaired quickly. Thus the manufacturer needs to provide local service.

UNIT 4

CHAPTER 6

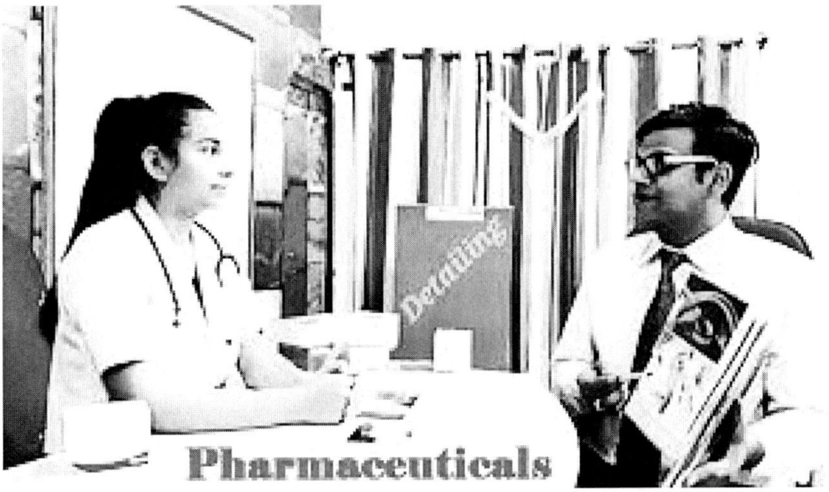

PROFESSIONALS SALES REPRESENTATIVE (PSR)

Personal selling involves face to face contact with a customer. There is direct interaction between the buyer and the seller. In this two way communication the seller can identify the specific needs and problems of the buyer and tailor the sales presentation in light of this knowledge.

In case of pharmaceutical products the personal selling involves doctors and chemists who contact with the patients. The sales person has to convince the doctors by his demander and presentations. The interaction should have reduced the risks that the doctor follow as its proper medication when administer to a patients.

Indirect personal selling is the dominant mode of communication for pharmaceutical products to doctors. In this case, there is high perceived risk of self purchase of the medicines because customer (patient) have lone level of product knowledge.

6.1 Professional sales representative (PSR)

A person who is engaged in selling goods to the customers is known as a 'salesman'. Professional sales representatives are generally convinced the physicians by describing their products benefit for prescribing the products to the patients. The medical representatives are supposed to describe the detailed prepared by the company marketing executives. The main objective of any business is to earn maximum profit and this is possible through maximum sales. Selling in the market is a tough job because of the stiff competition. It is necessary to create demand. Even the best product cannot be sold in the market until it is brought to the notice of the prospective buyers. PSR meet many doctors and they become familiar with various kinds of problems and suggest to their company's research department.

6.2 Duties of PSR

PSR calling on doctors cannot make a direct sale since the doctor does not buy drugs but prescribes them for patients. It is necessary to educate them. Personal selling or salesmanship is the oldest and most effective technique of selling. It is mostly done by PSR. Their duties are as follows:

(i) They help in understanding the use of the pharmaceuticals to the doctors.
(ii) They motivate change the buying behavior of the doctors
(iii) They can better understand the taste and attitude of the customers.
(iv) They help the manufacturers to designing the better products.
(v) They help in creation of a demand for new products.
(vi) They can develop durable relationship with consumers.
(vii) They demonstrate the products in a very effective way.
(viii) They try to remove the objections and doubts of a consumer.
(ix) They act as consultants to the physicians as well as pharmacists in the retailer.

6.2.1 Purpose of detailing

Pharmaceutical industry is rapidly growing industry and there is a big competition in the marketing of pharmaceutical products. Moreover pharmaceutical products are of different kinds by trade name but having same pharmacological actions. So product detailing is utmost necessary to the doctors.There are various purposes like:

(i) Detailing covers all the pertinent points which need emphasis.
(ii) It is prepared by professional experts at the head office of the company who need elaboration to doctors.
(iii) By this detailed representations the sale policy of company can be achieved.
(iv) The untrained medical professional can effectively present detailing to a doctor.
(v) Detailing helps whose lacks the normal vocabulary.
(vi) Detailing helps the physicians to understand the product application easily.

6.2.2 Different Stages of Detailing

(i) Approach: This is an important step in detailing. PSR enter the chamber of a doctor after taking his permission. Always exercise good manners while entering, seating, talking and even leaving the chamber of a doctor. They should put forward a question to the doctor in such a way that he gives an elaborate response. At this stage he starts the detailing of pharmaceutical products manicured by his pharmaceutical house with the help of visual aids.

(ii) Development of interest: It is very important for the success of detailing. The doctor will listen to the medical representatives only. Once MR knows about the needs of a doctor, the detailing should be done accordingly. The voice, expression should be enthusiastic in order to attract the attention of a doctor. Similarly the physical behavior of a person also expresses his feeling. Medical representative should always sit in an erect manner which indicates its enthusiasm and self-confidence.

(iii) Product name: In detailing the name of the product must be mentioned as many as it is possible. Normally it is necessary that PSR should mention the product name as frequently as possible, instead of referring to the specific product discussion as "it" or "our product".

(iv) Benefit of product: Once doctor is attentive and interested, PSR should start with main features and benefits of the product. He should talk only of patient benefit than to the product under discussion. While explaining the benefits according to features of the product, doctor can raise certain objections. These are a) prestigious objection) subjective objection c) unspoken objection d) last effort objection.

(v) Knowledge on drugs and cosmetic rules: Drug schedules help them processing of selling as per the type of drugs like general, antibiotic or habit forming drugs. Full schedule description is given below:

Schedules are the set of provisions for classifications of drugs, forms, fees, standards, requirements and regulations related to drugs and cosmetics under Drug and Cosmetic Act, 1940 and Rules, 1945. Here drugs includes pharmaceutical, Ayurvedic (including siddha), unani and tibb system of medicines, homeopathy etc.

Schedules are divided alphabetically and named also alphabetically like Schedule A, Schedule B etc till Schedule Y. Schedule Z is proposed but not implemented yet. Schedules are important part of Drug and Cosmetic Act 1940 & Rules, 1945. Every schedule contains specific information as discussed below.

Schedule A: Schedule A describes application forms and licenses types.

Schedule B: Schedule B describes Fees for test or analysis by the Central Drugs Laboratories or State Drugs Laboratories

Schedule B1: Schedule B1 describes fees for the test or analysis by the pharmacopoeial laboratory for indian medicine (plim) or the government analyst

Schedule C: Schedule C describes the Biological and Special Products

Schedule C(1): Schedule C(1) describes the Other Special Products

Schedule D: Schedule D describes the import requirements

Schedule D(1): Schedule D(1) describes the Information and undertaking required to be submitted by the manufacturer or his authorized agent with the Application Form for a Registration Certificate. The format shall be properly filled in for each application in Form 40. The detailed information, secret in nature, may be furnished on a Computer Floppy

Schedule D(2): Schedule D(2) describes the Information required to be submitted by the manufacturer or his authorized agent with the Application Form for the registration of a bulk drug/formulation/special product for its import into India. The format shall be properly filled in and the detailed information, secret in nature, may be furnished on a Computer Floppy

Schedule D(3): Schedule D(3) describes the information and undertaking required to be submitted by the manufacturer or his authorised importer/distributor/agent with the application form for a registration certificate

Schedule E(1): Schedule E1 describes the List of poisonous substances under the Ayurvedic (including Siddha) and Unani Systems of Medicine

Schedule F: Schedule F part I to Part XIIA were omitted. Part XII B describes the requirements for the functioning and operation of a blood bank and / or for preparation of blood components. partxiid describes the requirements for collection, processing, testing, storage, banking and release of umbilical cord blood derived stem cells.

Schedule F1: Schedule F1 is divided into parts. Part 1 describes about vaccines. Part 2 describes the antisera. Part 3- Diagnostic antigens which describes theschedule P.

Provisions Applicable to the Manufacture and Standardization of Diagnostic Agents (Bacterial Origin) . Part 4 – General.

Schedule F2: Schedule F2 describes the standards for surgical dressings.

Schedule F3: Schedule F3 describes the standards for umbilical tapes.

Schedule FF: Schedule FF describes the Standards for ophthalmic preparations.

Schedule G: Schedule G describes the list of drugs which are mostly in hormonal in nature.

Schedule H: Schedule H describes the drugs which can be sold out in retail against prescription of registered medical practitioner only i.e. prescription drugs

Schedule H1: Schedule H1 describes the drugs which can be sold out in retail against prescription of registered medical practitioner only. This schedule contains mostly antibiotics and habit forming drugs.

Schedule I: Schedule I has been omitted.

Schedule J: Schedule J describes the diseases and ailments (by whatever name described) which a drug may not purport to prevent or cure or make claims to prevent or cure.

Schedule K: Schedule K describes the class of drugs and extent & condition of exemption from provisions of Drug and Cosmetic Act, 1940 & Rules 1945.

Schedule L and L1: Schedule L has been omitted and Schedule L1 describes the good laboratory practices and requirements of premises and equipment

Schedule M: Schedule M describes the good manufacturing practices and requirements of premises, plant and equipment for pharmaceutical products.

Part 1: Good manufacturing practices for premises and materials.

Part 1A: Specific requirements for manufacture of sterile products, parenteral preparations (small volume injectable and large volume parenteral) and sterile ophthalmic preparations.

Part 1B: Specific requirements for manufacture of oral solid dosage forms (tablets and capsules).

Part 1C: Specific requirements for manufacture of oral liquids (syrups, elixirs, emulsions and suspensions).

Part 1D: Specific requirements for manufacture of topical products, i.e. external preparations (creams, ointments, pastes, emulsions, lotions, solutions, dusting powders and identical products).

Part 1E: Specific requirements for manufacture of metered-dose-inhalers (mdi).

Part 1F: Specific requirements of premises, plant and materials for manufacture of active pharmaceutial ingredients (bulk drugs).

Part 2: Requirements of plant and equipment

Schedule M-1: Schedule M1 describes the good manufacturing practices and requirements of premises, plant and equipment for homoeopathic medicines.

Schedule M-2: Schedule M2 describes the requirements of factory premises for manufacture of cosmetics.

Schedule M-3: Schedule M3 describes the quality management system –for notified medical devices and in-vitro diagnostics.

Schedule N: Schedule N describes the list of minimum equipment for the efficient running of a pharmacy.

Schedule O: Schedule O describes the standard for disinfectant fluids.

Part 1: Provision applicable to black fluids and white fluids

Part 2: Provisions applicable to other disinfectant fluids

Schedule P: Schedule P describes the life period of drugs.

Schedule P1: Schedule P1 describes the pack size of drugs

Schedule Q: Schedule Q describes the list of dye, colour and pigments

Part 1: List of dyes, colours and pigments permitted to be used in cosmetics and soaps

Part 2: List of colours permitted to be used in soaps

Schedule R: Schedule R describes the standards for condoms made of rubber latex intended for single use and other mechanical contraceptives.

Schedule R1: Schedule R1 describes the Indian Standards laid down from time to time by the Bureau of Indian Standards for medical devices.

Schedule S: Schedule S describes the standards for Cosmetics Standards laid down from time to time by the Bureau of Indian Standards.

Schedule T: Schedule T describes the good manufacturing practices for ayurvedic, siddha and unani medicines

Part 1: Good Manufacturing Practice.

Part 2: A-List of recommended machinery, equipment and minimum manufacturing premises required for the manufacture of various categories of ayurvedic, siddha system of medicines. B- List of machinery, equipment and minimum manufacturing premises required for the manufacture of various categories of unani system of medicines. C- List of equipment recommended for in-house quality control section. D- Supplementary guidelines for manufacturing of rasaushadhies or rasamarunthukal and kushtajat (herbo-mineral-metallic compounds) of ayurveda, siddha and unani medicines.

Schedule TA: Schedule TA describes form for record of utilization of raw material by ayurveda or siddha or unani licensed manufacturing units during the financial year

Schedule U: Schedule U describes the particulars shown in manufacturing records of drugs

Schedule U1: Schedule U1 describes the particulars shown in manufacturing record of cosmetics.

Schedule V: Schedule V describes the standards for patent or proprietary medicines

Schedule X: Schedule X describes the list of habit forming and narcotic drugs

Schedule Y: Schedule Y describes the requirements and guidelines for permission to import and / or manufacture of new drugs for sale or to undertake clinical trials

Schedule Z: Proposed

Case Study1

Presentation of Capsule Autrin: Doctor,anaemia is always a problem in medical treatment. Almost all your female patients must be suffering from iron. Chronic anemia must be treated before giving treatment to actual disease of the patient. Anemia patient have a feeling of tiredness, palpitation, tachycardia and body ache.

There are various preparations available in the market which acts as ferrous fumerate, vitamine $B_{12,}$ Vitamin C and folic acid. Iron is rapidly absorbed in ferrous form. So ferrous fumerate present in Autrin capsule is easily absorbed in presence of vitamins. More over ferrous does not cause constipation. It has no side effect and it is well tolerated both by pregnant and lactating women. Its retail price is reasonable and even your poor patients can afford to buy it. The recommended dose of Autrin is one capsule a day immediately after meals till hemoglobin content is improved. So Doctor may I count on your prescription for " CapsuleAutrin"

For recruitment, training and final selection of a professional sales representative, what process to be followed in this case study?

Answer- A competent and well experienced pharmacy professional shall be hired, for this following process to be followed.

Recruitment: is the process of searching prospective candidates to apply for jobs in the organization. It is the process to stimulate the prospective candidate to apply for the job. Its other purpose is to create a pool of candidates from which the most suitable persons may be selected for the job. A well-organized selection procedure has to be adopted to select suitable candidates for various jobs. The following selection procedure is generally adopted. So person should have professional qualification like B.Pharmor D.Pharm who can understand the application of vitamin C and folic acid etc.

(a) **Scrutiny of application:** The applications received up to date are carefully for various scrutinized. The incomplete applications and applications of candidates who do not fulfill the required eligibility conditions are rejected. Person should have sufficient selling experiences and communication skill.

(b) **Preliminary interview:** The candidate considered suitable on the basis of their application are called for preliminary interview. This is generally a brief interview and its purpose is to eliminate that candidate who is either unqualified or unsuitable for the job.

(c) **Selection test:** It may be written or an oral test depending of the number of candidates appearing for the interview. The technical and administrative capability can be judged from these tests. The psychological tests are very popular these days to judge human behavior in actual work situations. The following tests are commonly used in the selection process.

   (i) **Intelligent tests:** These tests are used to estimate the IQ or mental alertness of the candidate.

   (ii) **Aptitude tests:** These tests help to measure a candidate's capacity to learn particular skills and his potential abilities.

   (iii) **Trade tests-** these tests are designed to measure the applicant's level of knowledge and skill already achieved in a particular trade or occupation. These tests are also known as performance tests or proficiency tests.

   (iv) **Personality tests:** These tests are employed to find out the emotional balance, maturity, temperament of the candidate.

6.3 Challenges in selling the medicines by medical representative

(a) The face to face interaction between seller (medical representative) and indirect buyer (doctor) is very flexible but the flexibility comes at a cost.

(b) A sale on an average takes six visits but good sales person visit their clients (doctor) when they know that the client is not going to prescribe to his patient in the manufacturer.

(c) The nature of the personal selling function is changing.

(d) More and more companies are collecting purchase requests from their department and divisions and are buying from central locations.

(e) Few sales people sell products that are clearly superior to the competitors on most criteria. Sales people need to capitalize on what advantage their products have over similar competitive offerings.

(f) As buyer needs are becoming more complain sales persons need to be able to produce a package of products and services to provide a solution.

(g) It is difficult for a single sales person to sale to industrial customers. The application of medicines are complain and are of technical nature and the solution requires inputs from specialists.

(h) When there are no substantial difference between the product of the sale person and those of his competitors, the ability to provide services to the customer will clinch the deal for him.

6.4 Types of sales persons

(a) **Order taken:** Order taken are not expected to per made customers to buy the company's products or increase their quality of purchase. They are supposed to book customers order and pass on the information to relevant people in the company.

(b) **Inside order taken:** Retail sales assistants are typical inside order takens.The customer has full freedom to share products without the presence or influence of a sales person. Sales person rank is transactional.

(c) **Delivery sales person:** Delivery sales people are primarily concerned with delivery the product. There is little attempt to per made customers to increase order.

(d) **Outside order taken:** Sales person visits the customer; but they primarily respond to customer requests rather than actively seek to per made them.

(e) **Order creators:** The prime objective of order creators is to convince customers to buy the company's products. At same stage in the order getting process the sales person showed understand customer requirements and convince him that his company's products service his requirements best.

(f) **Order getters:** Order getters are industrial selling jobs where the major objectives is to per made the customer to make a direct purchase. These are front line sales people who are supported by technical support sales people and merchandisers.

(g) **New business sales people:** These sales person should maintain good relations with current customers who can provide them leads. They should also be prepared to make lot of cold calls and visits.

(h) **Organizational sales people:** These sales persons should be very sensitive to customer's problem on a day to day basis .They have to act as mediators between the customer and the functional departments of their own company.

(i) **Consumer sales people:** These sales people have to be sensitive of customer's time and they should not be insistent even when customer's have declined to buy. Seeing that a customer does not want the project it as important as sensing that the way want the company's product.

(j) **Technical support sales people:** These sales people have to support the customers during selling the products as products are highly technical operated. Financial specialists can provide the details technical and financial information required by customers.

(k) **Merchandisers:** They provide sales support in retail and wholesaling selling. Sales to individual outlets are supported by merchandisers who give advice on display, implement sales promotions and maintain contact with store managers.

6.5 Sales responsibilities

One of the most critical, issues the health care system facility is wrong medication. To avoid this role of medical professional is very import. So, the primary responsibility of a sales person is to increase sales at the same time they aware the physicians about its proper advice. Its first job is to identify the customers, presentation, and demonstration, handling objections and closing the sales. In order to generate sales since enabling functions should be carried out.

6.5.1 Prospecting

Sales team should always welcome a case for help from a customer as the team gets another opportunity to demonstrate its usefulness to the customer and semen its relationship with him.

6.5.2 Maintaining customer records and information feedback

Customers record keeping is an important activity for sales person who focus on getting repeat orders from their customers. Sales person should be encouraged to maintain data of finances of their customer requirements and behaviors. These records become very valuable when the key contact employee of a major customer leaves the company.

6.5.3 Providing services

After-sale services are also be givento the customer like product's incompatibility with the customer. What additional advantages he wants, or any modification to be expected that to be considered during manufacturing.

6.5.4 Handling complaints

During complaint handling top most priority should be give. To satisfy the customer is the main objective after selling of items. If the problem associated with the item,then it must be replaced immediately with a new item..

6.5.5 Journey routing

Top management Journey routing may be delegated to sales people. Many sales people believe that the most efficient routing plan involves a round trip approach, sales person should make adjust.

6.5.6 Relationship management

The management of relationship with key customer is a major responsibility of the sales person. It is a long-term nature. Buyers are also reducing the number of suppliers. The objective of relationship management is to build good will that is reciprocated by placing orders.

6.6 Personal selling skill

A good sales person lets the customer to talk. The sales person should first listen to the customer and then decorate his product. Success in selling comes from implementing the concept of customer orientation when face to face with consumers. A sales person will be successful when his conscious reason and passion and he will be a good motivator to make a sale. A sales person should not shy away from a customer in presence of sales person of a competitor.

Phases of selling process: Sales start with product knowledge up gradation of the sales person. With this knowledge, they face with the competitors and understand buyer behavior.

Product knowledge: Acquiring product knowledge means understanding both product features and customer benefits that they confer. The way the features turn into benefits is to view products from the customer's angle.

Competitor's product: This knowledge allows their strength to be offset against their weakness .It also helps the sales person to stress differential advantages of their products compared to competitor.

Selling call objectives: A sales person should net call objectives in terms of what the sales person wants customer to do rather than what the sales person should do.

6.6.1 Understanding buyer behaviors

Express gratitude: Never overestimate the customers. Always appreciate them for their purchase your product. Regular contact with them for future purchase. Ask their problems with the products.

6.6.2 Designing the sales force

Two critical decisions are determining sales force size and sales force organizations. Sales force size is decided by workload approach. Workload approach is based on calculation of total annual calls required per year divided by the average calls per year that can be expected from one sale person. It is defined as follows:

(i) customers are grouped into categories according to the value of goods brought and their potential for future.

(ii) Call frequency in number of calls per year to an account is assessed for each category of customers.

(iii) Multiply the call frequency by number of customers in each category to get the total number of calls that would be required to meet.

(v) Average number of calls that can be expected from a sales person is estimated.

(vi) Number of sales person = c/d.

6.7 Designing the Medical representatives (Medical Sales Executive)

Medical representatives are selling the medicines and diagnostic kits and health related devices to the patients through the doctor .Patients do not purchase the medicines directly from the medicine shop by law and by ethics. They solely depend on the prescription furnished by doctors. So the job of medical representative is more science based and they have sufficient knowledge of medicines and technical skills of application of the health devices. A medical representative is responsible for selling one or only a few related products of the company through a specialized doctor. It allows each MSR to be well informed about product (medicine) line, its application and patient briefers.

(i) They develop close relationship with doctor.

(ii) Doctors know that a dedicated medical representative exists to contact when a problem arises.

(iii) A competent medical representative can enables to create more in depth fluctuation of the decision making in choosing right kind of medicines.

6.8 Management of sales force

A large proportion of employees are engaged in sales activities efficiency and effectiveness of a sales force are very strong determinants of competitiveness of a company. High caliber sales people should be recruited. These are five stages of recruitment process.

(i) Preparation of job description and personal specifications. Top ten qualities sought for medical representative are communication skills personality, determination, intelligence, motivation, product knowledge, educational background, confidence, appearance, resilience and tenacity.

(ii) Source of requirement and method of communication.

(iii) Design of application.

(iv) Interview.

(v) Supplementary selection aids.

(vi) Training.

(vii) Motivation and compensation.

6.9 Types of sales persons

(i) Life style oriented: They try to maintain their standard of living by earning a predetermined amount of money. They do work accordingly to the type of life style they want.

(ii) Average performers: They perform at a level just sufficient to keep their job.

(iii) Trade off performers: They allocate their time base upon personally determined ratio between work and leisure that is not influenced by the prospect of higher caring.

(iv) Goal oriented: They prefer recognition as achiever by peers and superiors and tends to be sales quota oriented, with money mainly serving as recognition of achievement.

(v) Strictly money oriented: They want to maximize their caring. Family relationship, leisure may be sacrificed in pursuit of money.

6.10 Type of compensations:

1. **Fixed salary:** This is not liked to sales, Sales people are willing to carry out his or her duties on technical backup completing information feedback reports and prospecting. It provides security but opportunity to increase income by increasing sales.
2. **Commission only:** This provides a strong incentive to sell. There is unwillingness to take time off from direct selling tasks to attained training courses or fill in reports and there is high turnover.
3. **Salary plus commission:** This hybrid system provides some incentives sell with an element of security. The system is attractive to ambitious sales people who wish to continue a base level of income with the opportunity to earn more by greater effort and ability.
4. First three types of sales person will not be motivated by the commission opportunities but last two will be motivated with commission system.

6.11 Evaluation of sale people

Evaluation provides information to meet the targets and to guide them for training and motivation. Identification of strengths and weakness of each sales people and focused on areas in need of development and incentives for a poor prospecting performer.

(a) Quantitative measures of performance:

- (i) **Output criteria:** Output criteria based on sales revenue, profits generative, sales per active account,number of new accounts opened.
- (ii) **Input criteria:** Number of calls, calls per active account, calls on new account, number of prospects visited.

(b) Qualitative members of performance:

- (i) **Sales skills:** Questioning, make presentation.
- (ii) **Customers' relationship:** How much confidence do customers have in the sales person.
- (iii) **Product knowledge:** Proper application, its disposal system and storage condition.
- (iv) **Self management:** How well are calls prepared, routes organized.
- (v) **Co-operation and attitude:** To what extend does a sales person show initiative, follow instructions?

The use of quantities qualitative measures should be inter-related. A poor sales per call ratio will mean a close qualitative assessment of selling skills, customer relationship and product knowledge.

6.12 Features of a new medical representative/sales people

- (i) To understanding the customer's behavior.
- (ii) It has ability to convince the customer / doctor.

(iii) It should be intelligent in getting information.
(iv) It should be aware of the strategic objectives of the company.
(v) It should be enthuse to learn more about the company's as well as competitor's product.
(vi) Have low to more one place to another place with a great patience.
(vii) Can play a leadership role.
(viii) Should respect and trust the doctor and customers.
(ix) Must be accommodative and considerate to the need of the patients.

Other subsequent members are **distributors, retailers, wholesalers and medical representatives** who make the continuous flow of medicines to the patients.

6.13 Retailersduty

A retailer is a middle man between a wholesaler and actual consumer. Here the druggists acts as retailer and patient is the consumer. They always keep contact with wholesalers, manufacturer and the consumers. They have the following functions –

(i) Pharmacists keep a stock of various kinds of medicines according to the needs of the patients.
(ii) They are suppose to know the application of different kinds of medicines likely to be demanded by his patients recommendation by medical practitioners.
(iii) He also know the sources where the same could be obtained.
(iv) Retailer mainly make their own arrangement for transportation of products from the wholesaler go downs.
(v) Normally during storing gradation of goods are done by producer name or sometimes by wholesalers. However a retailer dose grading of those goods which have been left ungraded by the manufacturer and wholesalers.
(vi) Retailerhas to maintain a reasonable stock of goods. They bear the risk of loss of goods by fire,theft or deterioration as long as they are not sold.
(vii) Sometimes they provide financial help to consumers by selling them the goods on credit.
(vii) They keep close contact with their doctors who know the likes and dislikes of the prescribe medicines. In this regard marketing professionals (medical representatives) play an important role to convince the doctor. They pass on such information to the wholesalers for onward transmission to the manufacturers concerned.(mainly patient's complaints via doctor).
(viii) A retailer helps to promote the sale of goods manufactured by a particular manufacturer who has launched the sale promotion campaign by display the goods in show windows and on counter for the information of the customers.

6.14 Wholesaler duty

(i) Wholesaler communicates the customer's views about their products problems (merits and demerits) to the manufacturer.

(ii) Product advertising is mainly done both by the manufacturer and distributors.

(iii) Wholesalers are interested in the sale of popular products and they are not interested with the new product.

(iv) Wholesalers help the manufacturer to estimate the demand of their products in future, because they have a well knit network of retailers.

(v) Financial problems arise both from producers as well as retailers that can be eliminated by wholesalers. Retailers able to purchase goods on credit.

(vi) Free shop delivery is possible by wholesalers.

6.15 Medical Representative duty

They act as commission agents of the drug manufacturers. They sell goods on behalf of the seller. They negotiate with the doctors for prescribing their medicines and take the possession of the supplying the same in time through retailer. Mainly they do the following jobs.

(i) As they are qualified,gets intensive coaching and training on both product knowledge and selling processes. The success of a firm mainly depends on their performances.

(ii) They must have an attractive personality with goods health and sound physiques.

(iii) A pleasing and charming personality creates a good impression on doctors.

(iv) He must have the imagination to look at things from the view point of customer.

(v) He should possess a sound memory, presence of mind and imaginative power. He has a liking for people and ability to convince the doctors.

(vi) He has the patience to listen the various retailers and doctors to remove their objections.

(vii) He always be polite and courteous while dealing with his customers. Courtesy costs nothing but wins favor and permanent customers.

(viii) He must has specialized knowledge of selling techniques.

6.15.1 Function of a Medical Representatives

Pharmaceutical industries are rapidly growing and there is a big competition among the companies. The pharmaceutical products are similar in nature with varying of costs. Selling is largely depends on the potency of the sale forces. Detailing is a process of passing information of products manufactured by a pharmaceutical firm for prescribing their products by directly conversation with doctors.

Detailing is the main function of MR. It is done through the following processes:

Step I Approaching: MR enter the chamber of a doctor after taking his consent by sending the visiting card. He will create an environment in such a way that doctor pays undivided attention to him.Probing is the best tool to attract the attention of a doctor. Probing means to put forward a question to a doctor related to his patients or to his need. At this stage he should start the detailing of pharmaceuticals products manufactured by his pharmaceutical house with the help of visual aids.

Step II Development of interest: The development of interest is very important for the success of detailing.The doctor will listen to the medical representatives only if his talks are of any interest to him.Once the medical representative knows about the needs of a doctor, the detailing should be done accordingly. The voice of MR plays an important role. Similarly the physical behavior of a person also express his feeling. MR should always sit in an erect manner which indicates his enthusiasm and self confidence.

Step III Product knowledge: The name of the product must be mentioned as many as it is possible. The main aim is to visit a doctor to get him to prescribe the product by brand name.So medical representative should mention the product name as frequently as possible,instead of referring to the specific product discussion.

Step IV Benefits of the product: Once the doctor is attentive and interested,MR should talk only of the patient benefits and doctor benefits because the doctor is more concerned to the patient than to the product under discussion. While explaining the benefits according to the features of the product, doctor can raise certain objections. These objections are-

(a) **Prestigious objection:** It is raised by a doctor in order to show his medical competency. these objections have no scientific background. For example doctor may say "I am doubtful whether vitamin B_{12} is essential for the absorption of iron in the body."

(b) **Subjective objection:** It is raised according to the likes and dislikes of doctor. He may say that your cough syrup contains vanilla flavor which is not liked by his patients. These objections are raised depending on the likes and dislikes of different doctors.

(c) **Unspoken objection:** When doctors disagree with your detailing, doctor remain silent. It is very difficult to understand the reason of silence but try to understand his reason of silence and take necessary measures

(d) **Last effort objection:** Sometimes during detailing doctor raise objection which is not real objection. These are raise in order to avoid you. For example when MR try to request for an order, he just say that he has sufficient stock at this time or visit after a few days.

(e) **Closing:** Closing of detailing is very important. If medical representative does not close the detailing, he will loose.MR has done a difficult job to attract the attention of a doctor, created the interest, give briefing about the benefit of product, cleared all his doubts and convinced him.MR can close the detailing by two ways like demanding manner as well as requesting manner.

Case study 1

Organon India Limited,how they train their new employees?

A multinational Pharmaceutical company compulsorily conducting the employee training and induction program for all the new employees. Training primarily takes the form of mentoring and pairing new comers with seasoned representatives. New sales representatives are typically given two days to read the company hand book and then spend a week or two shadowing a senior sales representative before being assigned their own sales territories and quotas. A seven days program called " My First Week at Organon" is conducted to familiarize new recruits with the company's history, products, policies, payment plans, and product training as well as necessary functional skills.. The training program incorporated both an in-class training component and field-coaching sessions. A inspiring candidates have two days to absorb all the information provided to them including product specifications, demonstration information, and guidelines for prospecting and planning. Supplementary materials distributed during the program include a booklet detailing code of conduct and information on the system. Manuals are translated into the local languages.

Great importance is given to training, whereby diverse individuals are converted into a common entity. It can take years to build a connection and instill a recruit with knowledge and zeal, but the company only gets a few months to convert a raw 21 years- old, fresh out of school, into a true EuroCamp. A lot of things depend on this training, because unless the recruit learns well in the first few months, he can not achieve the goals of 60% sale target in the first six months, a prerequisite for going from probationary status to being confirmed.

Time constraints nevertheless occasionally preclude formal training beyond the two days it takes to digest reading materials. At such times, new champs are paired with a senior sales person and sent to "n in the field" . Training is an additional for the senior salesperson. Since he already has a lot of responsibility to complete each day, at times, training is handed in an informal manner. Within four to six months of joining, recruits participate in a second, more elaborative program, Making of a EuroCamp" that incorporate videos, role play and mock demonstrations.

Case study 2

Dabur India Limited,how they motivate their employees?

It is a fast growing pharmaceutical company holding a fourth rank in terms of sales among moving consumer goods(FMCG) companies in India in 2004.The company has a business in hair care, health care, oral care and foods. Dabur has ensured that the company's bottom line remains healthy over the years. This has been achieved due to the dedication of the all employees including the sale personnel.

Dabur, well-known for innovativeness of its promotion exercises, decided to utilize the popularity of Indian films in the domestic and global markets to promote its brands. In February 2004, Yash Raj Films Ad cell made 20 commercials for DaburChyawanpras and Hajmola with Amitabh Bachchan.He was signed on for Rs 80 mn., making this the most expensive advertising campaign undertaking by Dabur. He also endorsed Hajmola. The new campaign was in tune with the company's brand positioning of Hajmola as an " Anytime, Anywhere tasty, fun-filled digestive". Dabur capitalized on Bachchan's popularity in Bangaladesh, UAE,SaudiArabua, Kwait,Oman, Bahrain, Riyadh,Egypt and Nigeria as well. In 2004,the company signed cricketer VirenderSehwag and his wife as brand ambassadors for select oral,hair care and health care products. This was the first time a celebrity had been used for the oral care category with the turnover of Rs 100 crores.

The company planned to focus on Rassia and other CIS countries as well as in Afghanistan, West Indies and the Asia Pacific region. Dabur launched some export-specific brands like'Dr.Burman', where was launched in 2003 through multilevel marketing channels in Russia. In 2002-03, DaburBoro Glow was introduced for the Russian market and Vegecaps in the nature care range for the European markets. The company had been exporting hair oils, shampoos and Hajmola Candies to Afghanistan.

Case Study 3

Dr. Reddy's Labs, (DHL), how they well equipped their company?

Itis an Indian multination pharmaceutical company is well equipped with efficient and highly educated chemist. It has earned reputation as a leading generic drug company.DHL hired fresh Ph.D from universities and began grooming them for discovery research. In order to expand this talent pool, the company instituted "spirit of excellence" scholarships in selection India universities. Besides good salary and stock options, DRL's perks included financial support for attending national and international conferences, and encouragement for pursuing a doctorate while working for the company. There were also opportunities to work with foreign universities and hospitals

Money was raised in foreign capital markets to fund the company's diversification activities as well as to expand its generics business and support its new drug discovery efforts. The company's DGR issues in July 19194 netted 48 million dollar. It subsequently raised an additional 115.5 million dollar in the US market in April 2001 through an ADR issue, becoming the first non-Japanese Asian pharmaceutical company to be listed on the New York Stock Exchange.

Generics were the new growth segment for Dr. Reddy's Bulk activities and branded formulations provided the ballast. But both of these businesses were getting very competitive. Dr.Reddy's faced two businesses competitors in its bulk activities and branded formulations businesses, Rnbaxy and Cipla. The generics business a was also very competitive. Two of the largest generic companies, the Israeli Teva and Swiss Novaris Generics, only enjoyed 5.5 % market share each.

UNIT 5

CHAPTER 7

PRICING

7.0 Price

Price is negotiated between buyers and suppliers in business market. A buyer will be willing to pay a higher price for a product if it improves the buyer's functioning and profitability. Price negotiation is a common practice in business markets various tradeoffs in specifications and product service requirementschanging throughout the negotiation process. In most consumer markets customers generally accept or reject the price offered to them and very little negotiation is involved in the transaction. The price of the meniscus is determined by drug technical and price control board.

7.1 Domestic Market

Pricing depends on various factors like the types of consumers involved. The consumers in an individual or any business organization, price differs. A business house when buying a manufacturing machine must consider the lifetime costs and benefits of purchase. These might include factors like faster machine speed, high output, lower energy consumption, lower maintenance costs, lower repair costs, lower downtime for setup, greater functional flexibility higher resale price or lower disposal costs.

An intermediary in the distribution channel must consider how long a particular purchase will incur inventory costs. Business buyer consider the effects of technological obsolescence on purchases and the product's potential for adaptation, modification or upgrading as technological changes.

7.2 International market

The price is as high as

(i) There is additional cost of doing business in the foreign market.
(ii) Middle men involved.
(iii) Extra transportation cost needed.
(iv) Distribution channel may be very long.
(v) Extra cost of insurance, packaging shipping.
(vi) Varying rates of token and traffics in different market.

A company has to be successful in a foreign market if its offering have to be competitive in relation to domestic suppliers and other foreign suppliers. Before pricing its offerings a company will have to understand the price value equation of the customers of the foreign markets. A company will have to engineer the right value in its goods at a price the consumers in a foreign market are will to pay. Normally the price in the authorized distribution channel is higher and price in the unauthorized channel is lower.

Another phenomena concerning pricing in the international markets is dumping. Dumping is selling merchandise in another country at a price belong the price at which the same merchandise is sold in the home market or selling such merchandize below the costs incurred in production and shipment.

Transfer pricing refers to the price at which once division of a company sells products to another division of the same company. It concerns intra corporate exchange. Across border transfer pricing policies acquire complication. This can be fixed on the basis of cost of the product or on the basis of the market determined price or on the basis of negotiated price between the two units of the same company. However, the best method of setting transfer price is by using arun's length policy, whereby both the parties treat each other as independent, unrelated units and negotiate prices.

Another issue relates to nation levels in different countries. Company divisions that operate in high tax regimes sell at low prices to other divisions in low tax regimes, thus reporting less incomes and paying less tax. Those divisions that operate in low tax regimes sell at high prices to report higher incomes. Since taxation rates are despite having high incomes, such divisions end up paying less tax.

7.3 Pricing policies and objectives

Companies do their pricing in a variety of ways. In small companies, prices are often set by the boss. In large companies, pricing is handled by division and product live managers. Pricing is a key factor, every company will establish a pricing department to set or assist others in determining appropriate prices. This department reports to the marketing department, finance department or top management. Others who exert an influence on pricing include sales managers, production managers, finance managers and accountants.

7.3.1 Base on consumer psychology

Many economists assume that consumers are 'price taken' and except prices at 'face value' or as given understanding how consumers arrive it their perceptions of prices in an important marketing priority. There are three important prices namely

(a) Reference prices
(b) Quality inferences
(c) Price cues.

7.3.1.1 Reference prices

Consumers may have fairly good knowledge of the range of prices involved; company normally set the price of their product on the basis of reference prices. Clever marketers try to frame the price to singed the best possible value.

7.3.1.2 Price quality inferences

Many consumers use price as an indicator of quality. Image pricing is especially effective with ego sensitive products such as perfumes and expensive cars. Sometimes price act as a segued as quality.

7.3.1.3 Price cues

Consumer perceptions of prices are also affected by alternative pricing strategies. Many sellers believe that prices should end in an odd number. Pricing that end with '0' and '5' are also common in the market place as they are thought to be carrier for consumers to process and retrieve from memory.

7.4 Setting the price

A firm must set a price for the first time when it develops a new product, when it introduces its regular product into a new distribution channel or geographical area and when it enters bias on new contact work.

7.4.1 Selecting the price objectives

The clearer a firm's objectives, the carrier it is to set price. A company can pursue any of five major objectives through pricing

(a) Survival
(b) Maximum current profit
(c) Maximum market share
(d) Maximum market skimming.
(e) Product quality leadership.

7.4.2 Determining demand

Each price will lead to a different level of demand and therefore have a different impact on a company's marketing objectives. In normal case, demand and price are inversely related .In case of prestige goods, the demand curve sometimes scopes upward.

7.4.3 Estimating costs

Demand sets a ceiling on price the company can charge for its product. Costs set the floor. The company wants to charge a price that covers its costs of producing, distributing and selling the product; including a fair return for its effort and risks.

7.4.3.1 Types of costs

(a) **Fixed costs:** That does not vary with production or sales revenue.

(b) **Variable costs:** It vary directly with level of product.

(c) **Total costs:** It includes fixed and variable costs.

(d) **Average costs:** It is the cost per unit at that level of product. It is equal total cost divided by production.

7.4.4 Analyzing competitors

Analyzing competitors 'costs, prices and offers within the range of possible prices determined by market demand and company costs, the firm must take competitor's cost, prices and possible price reactions into account. The firm should first consider the nearest competitor's price.

7.4.5 Selecting a price method

Company normally select the price depending three costs the customers' demand schedule, the cost function and competitor's price . The major considerations in price setting are -

(a) Cost set a floor to the price.

(b) Competitor's price.

(c) The price of substitutes.

Companies select a pricing method that includes one or more of these three considerations. We will examines six price setting methods.

(i) Make up price

(ii) Target returns pricing.

(iii) Perceive value pricing.

(iv) Value pricing.

(v) Going rate pricing.

(vi) Auction type pricing.

7.4.6 Selecting the final price

Pricing methods narrates the range from which the company must select its final price. On selecting that price, the company must consider additional factors, including the impact of other marketing activities, company pricing policies gain and risk sharing pricing and the impact of price on the parts.

7.5 A few special pricing

(a) **Adapting pricing:** Company usually do not set a single price, but rather a pricing structure that reflect variations in geographical demand and costs ; market segment requirements, purchase timing, order levels,delivery frequency, guarantees, service contacts and other factors like discount, allowances and promotional support.

(b) **Geographical pricing:** In geographical pricing the company decides how to price its product to different customers different location and countries.

(c) **Discounts pricing:** Discounting pricing has become the modus operandi of a surprisingly member of companies offering both products and services. Sales people are quick to give discounts in order to close a sale. The discounts undermine the value perceptions of the offerings.

(d) **Promotional pricing:** Companies can use several pricing techniques to estimate early purchase. These are loss leader pricing, special want pricing cash rebates, lower payment terms, warranties and service contracts, psychological discounting .

(e) **Differentiated pricing:** Companies offer adjust their basic price to accommodate differences in customers, products, locations and so on .Land's, end creates men's flirts in many different style weight and levels of quality. These are customer segment pricing, product form pricing,image pricing, channel pricing, location pricing and time pricing .

7.6 An overview on Drug Price Control Order (DPCO)

Drug price control order 1966 was passed under section 3 of Essential Commodities Act 1955. It extends to whole of India. Under India's Drug (Pricescontrol) order, 2013, only the set of so-called "scheduled medicines" are under price control. There are no price caps on "non-scheduled medicines" that account for nearly 80 percent of domestic pharmaceutical market. However, the pharmaceutical department, citing market data that 89 percent of market for non-scheduled drugs have trade margin of less than 30 percent. Only 11 percent of the market of non-scheduled medicines has trade margins higher than 30 percent.

Manufacturing companies fix MRP_S of such non-scheduled medicines in such a way that there is generous amount of trade margin for wholesalers and retailers. There is a large differences between prices of medicines sold to distributors and MRP_S were imposing extra costs on patients.

The Government has been aware of this problem. It has promoted special shops where medicines are available without such high margins.

7.6.2 Calculation and fixing of price:

7.6.2.1 Bulk drug

The Government may from time to time fix the maximum sales price of the bulk drug in the first or second schedule. Encouragement to production from basic stage by way of higher rate of return by 4 %. Exemption from price control for production of new drug if developed through indigenous research and development.

7.6.2.2 Formulations

The retail price of the formulation shall be calculated in accordance with the following formula:

$$RP = (M.C. + C.C. + P.M. + P.C.) \times [1 + MAPE/100] + E.D.$$

Where,

RP = Retail price.

M.C.= Material cost.

C. C.= Conversion cost.

P.M.= Cost of packing.

P.C.= Packing charges.

MAPE = Maximum allowable posts –manufacturing expenses.

E.D.= Excise duty.

In the case of an imported formulation landed cost shall be considered.

Other methods of pricing

7.7.1 Full cost pricing

Cost based on variable and fixed cost per unit is added and the desire profit margin is added to the total cost. If sale/out-put goes down fixed cost per unit goes up, so price should go up. Therefore there is an increase in price as sale fall.

7.7.2 Direct cost pricing

The desire profit margin is added to the direct cost to obtain a price. Price does not cover full costs and the company would be making a loss. The strategy is valid if there is idle capacity.

7.7.3 Going rate prices

There is no product differentiation. All companies big or small charge the same price. This is not a attractive proposition for marketers. As margin is covering some part of fixes costs. It is useful for serving in period of low demand as they cannot be stored. It does not suffer from price up as demand goes down problem as it happens in full cost prices demand.

7.7.4 Comparative bidding

The usual process involves drawing up a detailed specification for a product and putting out for tender. Potential suppliers quote a price which is confidential to themselves and the buyers. A major focus for suppliers is the likely bid prices of competitors.

Expected profit = profit × probability of winning.

7.7.5 National Pharmaceutical Pricing Authority (NPPA)

National Pharmaceutical Pricing Authority National Pharmaceutical Pricing Authority (NPPA) constituted in 1997 is an independent Regulator for pricing. The National Pharmaceutical Pricing Authority was set up as an attached office of the Department of Chemicals and Petrochemicals (now Department of Pharmaceuticals since July, 2008) on 29th August 1997. It has been entrusted inter-alia, with the following functions.

(i) To implement and enforce the provisions of the Drugs Price Control Order (DPCO), 1995/2013 in accordance with the powers delegated to it.

(ii) To undertake and/or sponsor relevant studies in respect of pricing of drugs/formulations.

(iii) To monitor the availability of drugs, identify shortages, if any, and to take remedial steps.

(iv) To collect/maintain data on production, exports and imports, market share of individual companies, profitability of companies etc. for bulk drugs and formulations.

(v) To deal with all legal matters arising out of the decisions of the Authority.

(vi) To render advice to the Central Government on changes/revisions in the drug policy.

(vii) To render assistance to the Central Government in the parliamentary matters relating to the drug pricing.

7.8 Demand –supply laws

The price of the product largely depends on demand and supply laws of a product. According to Marshal Law of demand says "The law of demand states that other things being equal the amount demanded increases with a fall in price and reduced when price increases". This can be explained with the help of demand schedule.

Demand Schedule

Price (Rs)	Quantity (units)
10	100
9	150
8	200

The schedule shows extension of demand in response to decrease in price of commodity. Thus demand increases from 100 to 150 units, when price reduces from Rs 10 to Rs 9 per unit. The main assumptions of the law of demand are as follows:

(i) Taste and preferences of the consumers remain constant.
(ii) There is no change in the income of the consumer.
(iii) Price of the related goods do not change.
(iv) The wealth of the consumers does not change.
(v) Consumers do not expect any change in the price of the commodity in the near future.

7.9 How the demand to be increased

(i) When income of the consumer increases.
(ii) When price of the substitute goods increases.
(iii) When price of the complementary goods falls
(iv) When price of the commodity is expected to increase in the near future.
(v) When taste of consumer shifts in favor of commodity glue to change in fashion.
(vi) Increase In number of consumes

7.10 How the demand to be increased

(i) when income of consumer falls
(ii) When price of the substitute goods decreases
(iii) When price of complementary good increases.
(iv) When taste of the consumer shifts against the commodity due to change in fashion.
(v) When price of commodity is expected to decrease in the near future.
(vi) When the income of the consumer is expected to fall in near future.
(vii) When the number of consumers are decreased.

7.11 Other reasons

Demand changes due to quality of the product like i) normal goods ii) inferior goods iii) Giffen goods iv) Complementary goods v) substitutes.

(a) Normal goods: A normal goods is that goods whole income effect is positive and price effect is negative. Positive effect means that demand increases due to an increase in income and falls due to fall in income. Negative price effect means that a fall in price results in extension of demand and rise in price results in contraction of demand. The law of demand applies in case of normal goods.

(b) Inferior goods: An inferior good is that good whose income effect is negative. It means that an increase in consumer's income effect is negative. It means that an increase in consumer's income results in decrease in demand for that goods and a decrease in consumer's income results in an increase in demand for that good.

The main difference between normal goods and inferior goods is that the income effect of normal goods is positive while that of inferior goods is negative. Law of demand does not apply in this case.

(c) Giffen goods: These are those inferior goods whose income effect is negative but price effect is positive. In other words the demand for these goods rises due to a increase in price and fall due to decrease in price. Giffen goods are exception to the law of demand.

(d) Complementary goods: These are those related goods which jointly satisfy a particular want. In other words complementary goods are those goods where increase in price of one goods results in the fall in demand of other goods and decrease in the price of one goods results in the rise in demand of other goods.

(e) Substitutes: These are those goods which can be used in place of each other In other words substitutes are those goods, the demand of one is a positively related with the price of the other Arise in price of one leads to a rise in demand of other and a fall in price of one leads to fall in the demand of other.

7.12 Supply and law of supply

Supply indicates the actual requirement of goods and offered for sale at a given time, at various prices to the customers. It can be defined as the quantity of commodity offered for sale ar a given price in a given market at a given time. There are two types of supply:

(i) Individual supply

(ii) Market supply.

Individual supply refers to supply of a commodity by an individual firm in the market. Individual supply schedule expresses different quantities supplied by a firm at different prices

Market supply refers to supply of a commodity by all the firms in the market producing that particular commodity. Market supply schedule refers to supply schedule of all the firms in the market producing, supplying a particular commodity.

Factors affecting supply of commodity

(i) Price of commodity: There are direct relationship between prices of commodity and its quantity supplied. Higher the price, higher the quantity supplied. Lower the price, lower the quantity supplied.

(ii) Prices of all other goods: The supply of a good depends upon the prices of all other goods. An increase in the price of other goods makes them more profitable for the firm. They will increase their supply. On the other hand, the supply of the goods, the price of which has not changed, will become relatively less profitable. The supply of such goods may decrease.

(iii) Price of related goods: Related goods may be substitutes or goods of joint supplying opium and opium seeds. If the price of substitute rises its supply should accordingly increase. Likewise, the price of opium raises the supply of opium seeds should also increased.

(iv) **Number of firms-**It also depend on the total numbers of firm are supplying the good.Increase in number of firms there is more supply of goods in the market.

7.13 Roll of Supply chain management

The main function is to make the right product available to the right customer at right time. The retailer needs to manage the demand supply relationship effectively. This requires accurate and updated measurement system as well as efficient supply chain management. For this Management Information System (MIS) is developed. A suitable information technology system which will connect to their partners and form allies point of sale data for more credible of cash. It enables the retailer to store optimum at very day. Both customer and suppler will be benefited.

Case Study 1

The pricing policy of a company sends out signals about the company's philosophy. Customer's perceptions about the company and the brand image are considerably shaped by pricing.

Customers understand that companies have price flexibility. A company may choose to charge a lower price because it wants more people to own and enjoy its product. A company may never run a sales promotion to indicate that its product is always economically priced. A company may never indulge in bargaining and insist on fixed price to give the signal that argumentative customers will not have a better deal with the company. A company engaging in frequent sales promotion will give the signal that its prices cannot be trusted and customers only have to wait to get a lower price.

A company should be aware that the pricing strategies and tactics of the company send strong signals about the company's philosophies and beliefs.

Case Study 2

Profitability of high cost-to-serve customers should be periodically analyzed.

It is important to analyze whether returns from certain high profile customers are worth the cost to serve them. Most of these accounts are large, and demand product customization, just-in-time delivery, small order size and installation support while at the same time negotiating price very aggressively and paying late. These accounts demand and get more than what they pay for. Some of these accounts actually may be losing money.

High cost-to-serve customers can be very attractive if the prices they pay are high enough .It is always a good idea to check periodically whether each of these customers are yielding any profit at all.

Case Study 3

The marketer should be able to put monetary value to the benefits that the customer will derive from the product and price his product accordingly.

Companies which base the prices of their products primarily on their cost structures and on competitors' prices are essentially either taking great risk or are leaving lot of money on table. In one situation, the prices they arrive at may be perceived as too high in comparison to the product's benefit by customers and they may reject the product. In a completely reverse situation, a customer may be deriving lot of benefits from the product and would willingly pay a higher price if the marketer asked for it. Such situation can be avoided.

The marketer has to learn to put a monetary-value to the extra benefits that the customer will derive from the product in comparison to a competitor's product. For instance, a customer may expect to benefit 10,000 from higher quality and higher volumes if he buys the marketer's equipment .But the customer will have to spend 4000 for training the technicians and buying new fixtures. The marketer can charge a premium of 6000 (10,000-4000) for his product. He will pass on some of it to the customer to make the offer more attractive and charge a premium of 4000.

Case Study 4

Marketers should consider price sensitivity and transparency of buyers before setting prices.

In the eagerness to win a buyer's business in fiercely competitive environments, companies bid much lower than is required to take the buyer's business and leave a lot of money on the table. When companies analyze bids of competitors for orders that they eventually secured, they find that they quoted around 5-7 percent lower than next lowest bidder. Such situation arises because sales people report competitors' prices on the orders the company loses but not on those it wins. Such reports make the marketers believe that competitors always have the lowest prices, and in their anxiety to win orders quote very low prices when opportunities come to bid again.

Good marketers do not make such mistakes. They consider price sensitivity and price-transparency of the buyer before deciding their prices. When the customer's price sensitivity is high, the marketers matches or undercuts the competitors. But when the customer is bothered about other parameters like delivery or quality, the marketer enhances his offering on these parameters but prices it higher than competitors.

For a customer who showsevery competitor the price of other competitors, it is wise to price high so that competitors come to believe that the industry level is higher than it actually is. The marketer may lose some orders of transparent customers because of the higher price quoted but he will win many more since competitors are likely to quote higher prices in future due to their mistaken belief that the industry prices are higher. But when the customer does not reveal competitors prices to each other, it is safer to price lower and win the order.

UNIT 5

CHAPTER 8

EMERGING CONCEPTS IN MARKETING

8.1 Vertical and Horizontal Marketing

A vertical market is a market in which vendors offer goods and services specific to an industry, trade, profession, or other group of customers with specialized needs. An example could be software that manages services in hotels—amenities solutions.A vertical market is a particular industry or group of enterprises in which similar products or services are developed and marketed using similar methods (and to whom goods and services can be sold). Broad examples of vertical markets are insurance, real estate, banking, heavy manufacturing, retail, transportation, hospitals and government.

8.1.1 Characteristics of a vertical market

Customers in vertical markets have specialized needs and priorities. For example, law firms typically require software such as document management products tailored to their business processes. Additionally, law firms often have greater printing needs than other companies, making them a good candidate for managed printing services.

Specific regulatory compliance concerns also characterize vertical markets. Healthcare is one such highly regulated industry. Healthcare organizations must ensure they meet the requirements of legislation, including the Health Insurance Portability and Accountability Act (HIPAA) and the Health Information Technology for Economic and Clinical Health Act, or else they risk fines -- sometimes hefty ones. Other regulated industries include financial services and retail.Vertical markets can often be segment into narrower subcategories or niche markets. In theitality vertical market, for instant a vendor might target the subcategory of crucial ships.

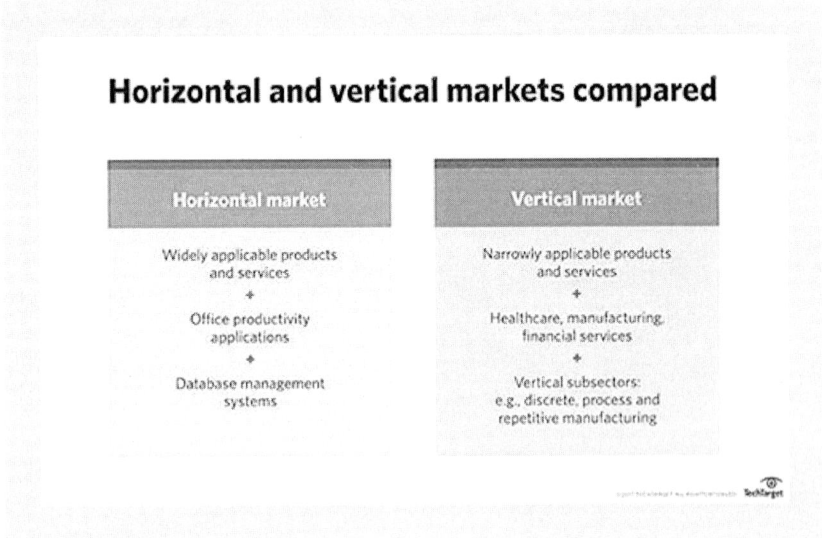

Horizontal market target more than one industry and a broad swath of clientele that share a general need. In terms of software, horizontal market products could include office productivity applications and databases.

8.1.2 Vertical marketing strategy

In the context of the IT channel industry, channel companies such as value-added resellers and managed services providers often choose to specialize in one or more verticals. To do so, channel companies look to gain experience and expertise in their targeted vertical market. This would include developing an understanding of that customer base's unique needs, business models and challenges, as well as the market's important trends and terminology. Additionally, companies that target vertical markets tailor their marketing plans and IT solutions to suit their targeted customer base.

8.2 Horizontal marketing

Definition: A Horizontal Marketing system is a form of distribution channel wherein two or more companies at the same level unrelated to each other come together to gain the economies of scale

A horizontal marketing system is a distribution channel arrangement whereby two or more organizations at the same level join together for marketing purposes to capitalize on a new opportunity. In other words, Horizontal marketing system is the merger of two unrelated companies who have come together to exploit the market opportunities.

Generally, this type of marketing system is followed by companies who lack in capital, human resources, production techniques, marketing programs and are afraid of incurring the huge losses. In order to overcome these limitations, the companies join hands with other companies who are big in size either in the form of joint venture –that can be temporary or permanent, or mergers to sustain in the business. Horizontal marketing system has gained popularity in the recent times due to an immense competition in the market where everybody is striving to gain a good position in the market along with huge profits.

In this marketing system, the collaboration can be between:

(a) Two or more Manufacturers: With an objective of making optimum utilization of scarce resources.

(b) Two or more Wholesalers: With the objective of covering a larger area of the distribution of goods and services.

(c) Two or more Retailers: With the objective of providing bulk quantities in a particular area.

Examples of Horizontal Marketing:

1. Nike and Apple have entered into a partnership, with the intent to have a Nike+ footwear in which the iPod can be connected with these shoes that will play music along with the display of information about time, distance covered, calories burned and heart pace on the screen.
2. Johnson & Johnson, a health care company, have joined hands with Google, with an objective of having a robotic-assisted surgical platform. That will help in the integration of advanced technologies, thereby improving the healthcare services.

Thus, two or more companies join hands to capitalize on the expertise of each and capture a greater market share.

8.3 Consumerism

Consumerism is the theory that states a country that consumes goods and services in large quantities will be better off economically. Sometimes, consumerism is referred to as a policy that promotes greed since it often promotes buying the latest and newest products.

8.3.1 Understanding Consumerism

Consumerism is driven by consumer spending, which can include buying cars, iPhones, and homes. Consumer spending is the driver behind over 60% of the economic growth in the U.S.As consumers spend, businesses benefit from increased sales, revenue, and profit. Companies, in turn, also spend money on manufacturing, computers, trucks, and hiring workers to satisfy the consumer demand for their products. The ancillary industries that supply businesses and consumers also do well. For example, if car sales are increasing, auto manufacturers will see a boost in profits. However, the companies that make the steel, tires, and upholstery for cars also see increased sales. In other words, consumerism can lead to benefits for the consumer but also the economy as a whole. Over-consumption and excess are also attributed to consumerism. For example, some people might argue that the Christmas holiday is a time of heightened consumerism, due to the large amounts of goods that are purchased during this time. At its core, consumerism postulates that the more materials acquired the better.

8.4 Rural Marketing

The rural consumer wants value for money primarily because he dose not have much money and he is looking for solution for basic needs. They look for endorsement by local leaders and heroes. The rural consumer's daily routine is relaxed and there is no sense of urgency in his lifestyle.They do not buy frequently and do not have plenty of surplus cash, his involvement level is high when he is purchasing as expensive product like a television. He is likely to do lot of consultation and will ask a lot of question before settling on a brand.

There are serious differences in consumer behavior depending on the caste and community of the rural consumer. Perceptions, traditions, and values vary from state to state. Even from region to region in a state. Thereforeit becomes important to carry out a detailed study of the attitudes and values of rural consumers of each region and for each product category. IT is not a good idea to extend the experience of one product category to another.

The communication should always be in local languages to capture the local spirit of the target rural customer. The communication must address the specific problems, needs, aspirations and hopes of rural consumers in each region. The rural consumer is rarely in hurry and the marketer should plan longer advertisements for rural consumer.

With all the talk of urbanization of rural consumers gaining prominence, it has become tempting to show the advertisements beamed to urban audiences to rural audiences too. The rural consumers may be visiting cities more often, their household may have a few gadgets and their children may be studying in cities, but rural consumers social milieu has not changed. Rural consumers will not understandclever, gimmicky. Fast-paced and sophisticated advertisements.They will not understand if the symbols, characters, and celebrities used in the advertisement are not directly related to the advertised product. Their world is still very much uncomplicated, and they receive simple, direct messages better than messages couched in abstract symbolisms.

8.5 Industrial Marketing

Industrial marketing, also known as business-to-business, marketing, is a branch of communications and sales that specializes in providing goods and services to other businesses, rather than to individual customers.

Industrial marketing (or business-to-business marketing) is the marketing of goods and services by one business to another. Industrial goods are those which an industry uses to produce an end product from one or more raw materials.

8.6 Global Marketing

India is the largest provider of generic drugs globally. Indian pharmaceutical sector industry supplies over 50 per cent of global demand for various vaccines, 40 per cent of generic demand in the US and 25 per cent of all medicine in UK.

India enjoys an important position in the global pharmaceuticals sector. The country also has a large pool of scientists and engineers who have the potential to steer the industry ahead to an even higher level. Presently over 80 per cent of the antiretroviral drugs used globally to combat AIDS (Acquired Immune Deficiency Syndrome) are supplied by Indian pharmaceutical firms.

8.6.1 Market Size

The pharmaceutical sector was valued at 33 billiondollar in 2017. The country's pharmaceutical industry is expected to expand at a CAGR of 22.4 per cent over 2015–20 to reach55 billion dollar. Pharmaceutical exports include bulk drugs, intermediates, drug formulations, biologicals, Ayush& herbal products and surgicals.

Indian companies received 304 Abbreviated New Drug Application (ANDA) approvals from the US Food and Drug Administration (USFDA) in 2017. The country accounts for around 30 per cent (by volume) and about 10 per cent (value) in the US$ 70-80 billion US generics market.

India's biotechnology industry comprising bio-pharmaceuticals, bio-services, bio-agriculture, bio-industry and bioinformatics is expected grow at an average growth rate of around 30 per cent a year and reach US$ 100 billion dollar by2025.

Case study 1

How does the physician prescribe the patient?

Mr RJ,a 67 years old retired plumber, has recently moved to your area and has come to the doctor to get his first prescription. He has a PMH of coronaryheart disease and has recently had an elective admission where drug eluting coronary artery stent was inserted. He has a long history of asthamawhich is well controlled with inhaled medicines.He does not want to stay long in the hospital

Answer

He has been advised to get admitted to hospital and useNuelin SA 500mg 12hourly(6am in the morning and 6pm in the evening). He response well to this treatment, but unfortunately after 2days of treatment he compel the doctor to get him relieve from the hospital. The clinical team is anxious to discharge him., so it is decided to give him a loading dose of aminophylline before releasing him for his better treatment.

INDEX

O

P

Q

R

S

T

U

W